Current
CONTROVERSIES

Domestic Surveillance

Other Books in the Current Controversies Series

Domestic Surveillance

Noël Merino, Book Editor

GREENHAVEN PRESS
A part of Gale, Cengage Learning

Farmington Hills, Mich • San Francisco • New York • Waterville, Maine
Meriden, Conn • Mason, Ohio • Chicago

Judy Galens, *Manager, Frontlist Acquisitions*

For more information, contact:
Greenhaven Press
27500 Drake Rd.
Farmington Hills, MI 48331-3535
Or you can visit our Internet site at gale.cengage.com

For product information and technology assistance, contact us at

Gale Customer Support, 1-800-877-4253
For permission to use material from this text or product, submit all requests online at www.cengage.com/permissions

Further permissions questions can be emailed to permissionrequest@cengage.com

Cover image Vasin Lee/Shutterstock.com

LIBRARY OF CONGRESS CATALOGING-IN-PUBLICATION DATA

Names: Merino, Noël, editor.
Title: Domestic surveillance / Noël Merino, book editor.
Description: Farmington Hills, Mich. : Greenhaven Press, [2016] | Series: Current controversies | Includes bibliographical references and index.
Identifiers: LCCN 2015021380| ISBN 9780737774344 (hardcover) | ISBN 9780737774351 (pbk.)
Subjects: LCSH: Espionage--United States. | Intelligence service--United States. | Privacy, Right of--United States.
Classification: LCC JK468.I6 D62 2016 | DDC 363.325/1630973--dc23
LC record available at http://lccn.loc.gov/2015021380

Printed in Mexico
1 2 3 4 5 6 7 19 18 17 16 15

Contents

Chapter 2: How Does Domestic Surveillance Affect Privacy and Security?

Chapter 3: Is Domestic Surveillance Constitutional?

Yes: Domestic Surveillance Is Constitutional

The US Constitution and the Patriot Act, passed after the 9/11 terrorist attacks, allow the government to protect national security through intelligence gathering, such as that being conducted by the National Security Agency. These activities are rigorously monitored by Congress and the courts, and to date there has been no evidence of abuse.

No: Domestic Surveillance Is Not Constitutional

Chapter 4: How Should Government Surveillance Be Regulated?

The National Security Agency's mass collection of telephone call-records data should not be further limited or altered as proposed by the President's Review Group on Intelligence and Communications Technologies. Such changes, like having the database held by a third party rather than the NSA, would greatly undermine the usefulness of the program.

Foreword

By definition, controversies are "discussions of questions in which opposing opinions clash" (*Webster's Twentieth Century Dictionary Unabridged*). Few would deny that controversies are a pervasive part of the human condition and exist on virtually every level of human enterprise. Controversies transpire between individuals and among groups, within nations and between nations. Controversies supply the grist necessary for progress by providing challenges and challengers to the status quo. They also create atmospheres where strife and warfare can flourish. A world without controversies would be a peaceful world; but it also would be, by and large, static and prosaic.

The Series' Purpose

The purpose of the Current Controversies series is to explore many of the social, political, and economic controversies dominating the national and international scenes today. Titles selected for inclusion in the series are highly focused and specific. For example, from the larger category of criminal justice, Current Controversies deals with specific topics such as police brutality, gun control, white collar crime, and others. The debates in Current Controversies also are presented in a useful, timeless fashion. Articles and book excerpts included in each title are selected if they contribute valuable, long-range ideas to the overall debate. And wherever possible, current information is enhanced with historical documents and other relevant materials. Thus, while individual titles are current in focus, every effort is made to ensure that they will not become quickly outdated. Books in the Current Controversies series will remain important resources for librarians, teachers, and students for many years.

In addition to keeping the titles focused and specific, great care is taken in the editorial format of each book in the series. Book introductions and chapter prefaces are offered to provide background material for readers. Chapters are organized around several key questions that are answered with diverse opinions representing all points on the political spectrum. Materials in each chapter include opinions in which authors clearly disagree as well as alternative opinions in which authors may agree on a broader issue but disagree on the possible solutions. In this way, the content of each volume in Current Controversies mirrors the mosaic of opinions encountered in society. Readers will quickly realize that there are many viable answers to these complex issues. By questioning each author's conclusions, students and casual readers can begin to develop the critical thinking skills so important to evaluating opinionated material.

Current Controversies is also ideal for controlled research. Each anthology in the series is composed of primary sources taken from a wide gamut of informational categories including periodicals, newspapers, books, US and foreign government documents, and the publications of private and public organizations. Readers will find factual support for reports, debates, and research papers covering all areas of important issues. In addition, an annotated table of contents, an index, a book and periodical bibliography, and a list of organizations to contact are included in each book to expedite further research.

Perhaps more than ever before in history, people are confronted with diverse and contradictory information. During the Persian Gulf War, for example, the public was not only treated to minute-to-minute coverage of the war, it was also inundated with critiques of the coverage and countless analyses of the factors motivating US involvement. Being able to sort through the plethora of opinions accompanying today's major issues, and to draw one's own conclusions, can be a complicated and frustrating struggle. It is the editors' hope that Current Controversies will help readers with this struggle.

Introduction

"There are constitutional protections from certain surveillance activities and laws governing permissible surveillance, though what is permissible is often in flux—or even up in the air—due to changing technology."

Surveillance is the act of observing people with or without their knowledge. Government surveillance is conducted as a regular part of law enforcement and national security. For example, suspected criminals may have their phone conversations monitored by law enforcement, and suspected foreign terrorists may have their e-mail and Internet activity monitored by the National Security Agency (NSA). However, there are constitutional protections from certain surveillance activities and laws governing permissible surveillance, though what is permissible is often in flux—or even up in the air—due to changing technology.

The Fourth Amendment to the US Constitution creates individual rights regarding searches and seizures. It reads:

> The right of the people to be secure in their persons, houses, papers, and effects, against unreasonable searches and seizures, shall not be violated, and no Warrants shall issue, but upon probable cause, supported by Oath or affirmation, and particularly describing the place to be searched, and the persons or things to be seized.

The Fourth Amendment guarantees those in the United States freedom from searches and seizures by government officials when such activity is not justified by probable cause. The definition of probable cause and, thus, the conditions under which individuals may be searched has been defined and redefined over the years by the US Supreme Court's decisions.

The Supreme Court has defined reasonable searches to be limited by expectations of privacy: although there is little expectation of privacy in public or in one's car, there is an expectation of privacy in one's home and of one's body. In general, the Court has determined that before individuals or their property can be legally searched by law enforcement, a warrant must be obtained from a judge. Nonetheless, there are numerous exceptions to the warrant requirement, such as when an individual consents to a search, when the search is solely to screen for weapons, when the search is at the border, or when the search is deemed immediately necessary for public safety.

With respect to electronic surveillance—a search under the meaning of the Fourth Amendment—there are restrictions on the information law enforcement may collect, but there are often exceptions. The Wiretap Act of 1968 established that for legal domestic wiretapping of wire, oral, or electronic communications, government must establish probable cause of crime and show that wiretapping is necessary for law enforcement. The Electronic Communications Privacy Act (ECPA) of 1986 updated the Wiretap Act to include new technologies. Nonetheless, the Foreign Intelligence Surveillance Act (FISA) of 1978 authorized electronic surveillance for specific foreign intelligence purposes (applying to foreigners within the United States and US citizens who are terrorist suspects), both without court orders and with court orders from the specially created FISA court.

Privacy protections established by the Fourth Amendment, the Wiretap Act, and ECPA have been limited by recent legislation aimed at improving the ability of law enforcement and national security organizations to conduct surveillance in the name of national security. The Communications Assistance for Law Enforcement Act of 1994 required telecommunications companies to create built-in mechanisms for government surveillance. The USA PATRIOT Act, passed shortly after the terrorist attacks of September 2001, expanded legal surveillance procedures for the purposes of preventing terrorism. The FISA Amendments Act of 2008 authorized the surveillance of foreigners abroad and, with FISA court permission, surveillance of Americans abroad.

In spring 2013, former NSA contractor Edward J. Snowden released documents showing that the NSA had engaged—and continued to engage—in widespread surveillance not only of foreigners but also of Americans, both at home and abroad. The news of such widespread surveillance created controversy both within and outside the United States, spawning debate over the proper scope of Fourth Amendment protection and the balance between privacy and security.

American opinion of NSA surveillance has varied over time. According to various *Washington Post*-ABC News polls, large majorities have supported government surveillance following the terrorist attacks of September 11, 2001, viewing such surveillance as necessary to protect national security. That majority shrunk to 57 percent after Snowden revealed the news of domestic NSA surveillance. Nonetheless, several days after the Paris terrorist attacks in January 2015, polling revealed that 63 percent of Americans felt that it was acceptable to give up a certain amount of personal privacy to let the government investigate terror threats. Regardless, Americans across the board show less support for surveillance of Americans domestically than when it is conducted on foreigners abroad.

Due to the secrecy of NSA surveillance, there are limits on what the public knows about the government's surveillance programs. There exists opposing viewpoints on whether or not domestic surveillance is a problem and the extent to which it needs to be curtailed. Various commenters, politicians, and experts debate these issues and others in *Current Controversies: Domestic Surveillance*, shedding light on this ongoing social debate.

CHAPTER 1

Is Domestic Surveillance a Problem?

Few See Adequate Limits on NSA Surveillance Program, But More Approve than Disapprove

Pew Research Center

The Pew Research Center is a nonpartisan fact tank that informs the public about the issues, attitudes, and trends shaping America and the world.

A majority of Americans—56%—say that federal courts fail to provide adequate limits on the telephone and internet data the government is collecting as part of its anti-terrorism efforts. An even larger percentage (70%) believes that the government uses this data for purposes other than investigating terrorism.

And despite the insistence by the president and other senior officials that only "metadata," such as phone numbers and email addresses, is being collected, 63% think the government is also gathering information about the content of communications—with 27% believing the government has listened to or read *their* phone calls and emails.

Nonetheless, the public's bottom line on government anti-terrorism surveillance is narrowly positive. The national survey by the Pew Research Center, conducted July 17–21 among 1,480 adults, finds that 50% approve of the government's collection of telephone and internet data as part of anti-terrorism efforts, while 44% disapprove. These views are little changed from a month ago, when 48% approved and 47% disapproved.

The divisions in public opinion about the government's data-collection program were mirrored in a congressional vote this week on the issue. On July 24, the House of Representatives narrowly defeated an amendment to scale back the NSA's telephone data collection.

Overall, 47% say their greater concern about government anti-terrorism policies is that they have gone too far in restricting the average person's civil liberties.

Nationwide, there is more support for the government's data-collection program among Democrats (57% approve) than among Republicans (44%), but both parties face significant internal divisions: 36% of Democrats disapprove of the program as do 50% of Republicans.

While views of the program itself are mixed, the debate has raised public concern about whether anti-terror programs are restricting civil liberties.

Overall, 47% say their greater concern about government anti-terrorism policies is that they have gone too far in restricting the average person's civil liberties, while 35% say they are more concerned that policies have not gone far enough to protect the country. This is the first time in Pew Research polling that more have expressed concern over civil liberties than protection from terrorism since the question was first asked in 2004.

As concern about civil liberties has grown, the issue now divides members of both parties. Roughly four-in-ten Republicans (43%) and Democrats (42%) say their greater concern over anti-terror policies is that they have gone too far in restricting civil liberties, up sharply from three years ago (25% and 33% in 2010, respectively).

Republicans and Democrats also express similar opinions about news coverage of secret government anti-terrorism programs: Nearly identical percentages in both parties (45% of

Democrats, 43% of Republicans) say that the news media should report information it obtains about the secret methods the government uses to fight terrorism, while 51% in each party say it should not.

This marks a change in opinion among both parties since 2006, when Bush administration anti-terror surveillance programs faced scrutiny. In May 2006, a Gallup/USA Today poll found that most Democrats supported news reporting on secret anti-terror programs, while most Republicans said the press should not divulge this information.

A broad majority of the public (70%) believes that the government . . . is using the data it collects through the NSA program for purposes other than to investigate terrorism.

Many Who Think Gov't Has Accessed *Their* Data Support the Program

The public's views of the government's anti-terrorism efforts are complex, and many who believe the reach of the government's data collection program is expansive still approve of the effort overall. In every case, however, those who view the government's data collection as far-reaching are less likely to approve of the program than those who do not.

People who believe the government is collecting what is actually being said in emails and phone calls are divided over the overall program: About as many approve (47%) as disapprove (50%) of the government's collection of phone and internet data as part of anti-terrorism efforts despite the impression that it is not limited to metadata.

Even among those who believe *their own* communications have been read or listened to, 40% approve of the program, while 58% disapprove.

Of those who say the government is using data for purposes other than to investigate terrorism, 43% approve of the government's data collection; 53% disapprove. Among the small minority (22% of the public) that says the data is only being used to investigate terrorism, 71% approve while just 23% disapprove.

And those who say federal courts do not place adequate limits on the information the government can collect disapprove of the program by a 62%-36% margin. Conversely, those who say there are adequate limits approve of it, 75%-21%.

Some Suspect Political Motives in Use of Data

A broad majority of the public (70%) believes that the government also is using the data it collects through the NSA program for purposes other than to investigate terrorism. When those who express this view are asked an open-ended question about what other purposes the data is being used for, a range of responses are given, with many focusing on general concerns about government monitoring and spying.

About two-in-ten (19%) say the government is using this data to spy or "be nosy," and another 14% say it is being used for general purposes or monitoring.

But some say the government is collecting this data for political purposes: 13% say the government has a political agenda, while another 5% say it is being used for general profiling or targeting, to target interest and religious groups or for tax purposes.

Rising Concern over Civil Liberties

Nearly half of Americans (47%) say their greater concern about government anti-terrorism policies is that they have gone too far in restricting the average person's civil liberties; 35% say their greater concern is that they have not gone far enough to adequately protect the country. There has been a 15-point rise in the percentage saying their greater concern is civil liberties since Pew Research last asked the question in October 2010. This is the first time a plurality has expressed greater concern about civil liberties than security since the question was first asked in 2004.

The increase in concern about civil liberties has taken place across the board, with double-digit shifts in opinion among nearly all partisan and demographic groups. Republicans prioritized security over civil liberties by a 58%-25% margin in 2010. Today, Republicans are as likely to say their bigger concern is civil liberties (43%) as security (38%), a balance of opinion nearly identical to that among Democrats (42% civil liberties, 38% security).

Those under the age of 30 stand out for their broad concern over civil liberties.

While this change has been broad-based, the transformation among Tea Party Republicans stands out. Today, most Republican and Republican-leaning independent voters who agree with the Tea Party are more concerned that government programs are going too far in restricting civil liberties (55%). In October 2010, Tea Party Republican voters by about three-to-one (63% to 20%) said the programs did not go far enough in protecting the country.

Among Democrats and independents, increasing percentages also say their greater concern is that anti-terror policies have curbed civil liberties. About four-in-ten Democrats (42%) express this view, up from 33% three years ago. And the share of independents expressing greater concern over civil liberties has risen 17 points since 2010.

Those under the age of 30 stand out for their broad concern over civil liberties. By about two-to-one (60%-29%) young people say their bigger concern about the government's anti-terrorism policies is that they have gone too far in restricting the average person's civil liberties rather than not going far enough to protect the country.

There is also a substantial gender gap: by a 51% to 29% margin men are more concerned that government policies have gone too far in restricting civil liberties. Women are divided, with 42% more worried about civil liberties and 40% more concerned that government policies haven't gone far enough to protect the country.

The Secret Surveillance State Threatens Freedom

Dan Verton

Dan Verton is a technology journalist covering the federal government and the author of several books on cybersecurity.

How did it come to this?

How did [President] Barack Obama's promise of hope and change, which led the nation to reject the paranoid neoconservative view of the world, become a never-ending Orwellian nightmare in which Americans must now accept the secret machinations of an intelligence industrial complex, lest we be attacked by terrorists?

A Manufactured Paranoia

Many Americans, particularly those familiar with the language contained in the Fourth Amendment to the Constitution that provides for protections against unreasonable searches and seizures, are asking that very question in the wake of the revelations that the FBI [Federal Bureau of Investigation] and National Security Agency (NSA) have been tracking phone calls and Internet usage of tens of millions of Americans.

As with the answers to the most difficult questions pertaining to homeland security and counterterrorism, all roads lead back to 9/11 and a damaged American psyche that seems to be willing to accept almost any encroachment by the state in the name of security.

The government's decade-long effort to systematically erode the privacy protections contained in the Constitution has finally succeeded because Americans have allowed it to happen. Contrary to the multitude of technology pundits who claim such programs are a natural outgrowth of the digital economy—an evolution, they say, we are powerless to stop— the real issue at play is the ultra secretive nature of government decision making on matters that impact the nature of our democratic system. And central to that secrecy is a manufactured paranoia that seeks to convince us that we must accept these decisions or we will be killed by terrorists.

Americans never got to make the choices Obama speaks of because the state made them for us.

In his defense of the programs—delivered like a child rationalizing why he was caught with his hand in the cookie jar—Obama said the nation must "make some choices as a society" when it comes to balancing our irrational desire for total security with our fundamental rights as Americans. Members of Congress and the leaders of the intelligence community jumped right onto the balance bandwagon, telling us that on multiple occasions we weren't killed because of what Obama called a "modest" encroachment on our privacy.

The one exception worthy of mention here is, of course, Rep. Peter King (R-NY), who not only seems willing to spy on all Americans, but also seems eager to destroy the nation's tradition of a free press by jailing responsible journalists.

Surveillance Created in Secret

But no real details outlining the programs' success have been provided, because the programs are secret. Americans never got to make the choices Obama speaks of because the state made them for us. The state decided what the acceptable balance was between security and liberty. Some point to safeguards, like informing Congress and requiring court approval. But how much protection should Americans reasonably expect from representatives like King who see terrorists around every corner and want to jail journalists, and a secret court that abides by procedures only the state understands?

Ten years after the 9/11 terrorist attacks—that seminal event in American history that our leaders pledged would not change our way of life—we now live under a de facto surveillance society managed not only by the pure-hearted capitalists in our midst, but by the state as well. America today quite literally has a camera on nearly every street corner, and now a government computer taking note of every phone call, Web site visit, and social interaction on the Internet.

Such a society would be fundamentally un-American in the best of times. But in the worst of times—times of unending war and constant fear-mongering—such a society has the capacity to fundamentally alter what it means to be an American and how people act in a "free" society.

America faces real threats and secrets are necessary. But Americans have the right to choose what the nature of our democracy will be in these challenging times. And it is no longer a free and democratic society when elected officials and bureaucrats get to make that choice for us in complete secrecy.

Surveillance Is a Problem Even If Americans Acquiesce

Elizabeth Goitein

Elizabeth Goitein codirects the Brennan Center for Justice's Liberty and National Security Program at New York University School of Law.

Little by little, Americans are allowing their government to chip away at the fortress of legal protections that people in less-privileged societies—including multiple nations in the Arab world—are giving their lives to build.

The Public's Reaction to Surveillance

The director of National Intelligence today [July 31, 2013] declassified and released documents describing the National Security Agency's (NSA) "bulk collection" of Americans' telephone records as taking place "on a very large scale." Last week, the House of Representatives voted by a razor-thin margin to allow this practice to continue. The vote aptly reflects Americans' polarized response to revelations about the NSA's activities. Half the country is incensed by the secret spying. The other half, however, appears to have heeded Senate Majority Leader Harry Reid's now-famous advice to "just calm down and understand that this isn't anything that is brand new."

Among this latter group, there is a sense that privacy advocates are making much ado about nothing. The NSA's data collection programs were approved by federal judges; Congress knew about them; they're used only to identify terrorists. What, exactly, is the big deal?

The most obvious answer is that these programs may be illegal. The government admits it obtains Americans' telephone records in bulk, but claims officials do not examine them unless there is reason to suspect a terrorist link. Section 215 of the Patriot Act, however, requires the government to establish a record's investigative relevance before obtaining it—not after. The PRISM program, which collects information from Internet service providers, is ostensibly legal because it "targets" foreigners. But the program tolerates extensive "inadvertent" and "incidental" collection of Americans' information—including information the government needs a warrant to obtain under the Fourth Amendment.

The government knows very well how revealing call records can be; that is why it considers the program so valuable.

Yes, a secret court approved these programs. That should not start and end the discussion about their legality. Judges make mistakes, and—as recent reporting on the secret Foreign Intelligence Service Act (FISA) Court has underscored—they are far more likely to do so when they hear only the facts and arguments that one side chooses to present. When citizens have gone to the regular courts to challenge government surveillance, the government has successfully argued that the courts cannot even consider their claims.

The programs also threaten Americans' privacy. It is disingenuous for officials to characterize the "metadata" being collected as mere phone numbers. Sophisticated computer programs can glean volumes of sensitive information from this metadata about people's relationships, activities, and even beliefs. The government knows very well how revealing call records can be; that is why it considers the program so valuable.

A Dangerous Trend

Serious as they are, these concerns fail to explain fully why Americans should care. After all, this remains a remarkably free country. There are exceptions. Muslim Americans, who are singled out for scrutiny by some law enforcement agencies, have reported harassment by customs officials as well as a chilling of political and religious activity. Outside of these communities, though, few Americans feel any tangible effects from increased surveillance. The vast majority of law-abiding citizens go about their lives without fear of government persecution.

And that may be the problem. Free societies tend to take their freedom for granted. But our liberties do not derive from the innate trustworthiness of our elected representatives. They derive from laws and institutions put in place for the preservation of liberty. These laws and institutions, some version of which can be found in all democratic societies, are relatively recent innovations in human history. Before their advent, tyrannies and dictatorships were the norm. Even today, in countries without this framework, people are not free.

Each additional broadening of the government's powers must be a matter of choice—not passive acquiescence to a secret expansion.

Since 9/11, the laws and institutions created to ensure Americans' freedom have been weakened—sometimes incrementally, sometimes significantly—at a rapid pace. This is particularly true for limitations on surveillance, a power that carries tremendous potential for abuse. National Security Letters, a form of administrative subpoena, are now available to collect any information "relevant" to a terrorism investigation, not just information about potential suspects. Customs agents no longer need reasonable suspicion of wrongdoing to search citizens' laptops at the border. Americans' international communications are now subject to wiretapping without an individualized court order. The list goes on.

In any given instance, the government can make the case that the change is small, or that it is justified by increased security. In some cases, the argument may be persuasive. It is the trend, however, that should concern us. Twelve years after 9/11, as the nation approaches the date for withdrawing troops from Afghanistan, the quiet erosion of Americans' civil liberties continues.

That doesn't mean the US government should never expand surveillance authorities, or that Americans should resolve all trade-offs between liberty and security in favor of liberty. After all, the United States is a long way from a dictatorship. But given the post-9/11 trend of diminishing legal protections, Americans should not make these choices lightly. And each additional broadening of the government's powers must be a matter of choice—not passive acquiescence to a secret expansion. When that choice is taken from the citizenry, it is no occasion to "calm down" and look the other way.

Americans Are Comfortable with Expanded Domestic Surveillance

Dan Murphy

Dan Murphy is a staff writer for the Christian Science Monitor's *international desk, focused on the Middle East.*

A Pew Research Center poll conducted from June 6 to 9 [2013], prompted by revelations of an extensive domestic surveillance program involving the National Security Agency [NSA], found that a large number of US citizens are comfortable with trading privacy for security.

The Overall Picture

The poll found that 56 percent of Americans considered it "acceptable" for the NSA to get "secret court orders to track calls of millions of Americans to investigate terrorism," while 41 percent of those surveyed found this "not acceptable."

This was the first time Pew had asked that specific question. It has asked the question "should the government be able to monitor everyone's e-mail to prevent possible terrorism" for a number of years. For that proposition there is less support, perhaps because it doesn't include any judicial oversight. In 2002, 45 percent said they supported e-mail monitoring, while 47 percent said they didn't support that. In June 2013, 45 percent still indicated they supported e-mail monitoring, but the number of Americans opposed to it rose to 52 percent.

The overall picture is still one in which large numbers of Americans are deeply frightened by terrorism and want the government to devote significant resources to combat it, not-withstanding the fact that terrorism is not much of an actual threat. On balance, most people polled indicated security is more important to them than privacy, which is the reason that expanded surveillance powers and the use of secret courts have been so popular among lawmakers.

> *The way the attitudes of Democrats and Republicans have shifted on the issue [of surveillance] since President Obama took office is once again evidence of the power of partisanship, rather than principle, in how voters see the world.*

Pew writes:

Currently 62% say it is more important for the federal government to investigate possible terrorist threats, even if that intrudes on personal privacy. Just 34% say it is more important for the government not to intrude on personal privacy, even if that limits its ability to investigate possible terrorist threats.

These opinions have changed little since an ABC News/Washington Post survey in January 2006. Currently, there are only modest partisan differences in these opinions: 69% of Democrats say it is more important for the government to investigate terrorist threats, even at the expense of personal privacy, as do 62% of Republicans and 59% of independents.

The polling did find a meaningful gap between older and younger Americans on this issue, with older Americans being less concerned about privacy.

"While six-in-10 or more in older age groups say it is more important to investigate terrorism even if it intrudes on privacy, young people are divided: 51% say investigating terrorism is more important while 45% say it is more important for the government not to intrude on personal privacy, even if that limits its ability to investigate possible threats," Pew writes.

The Impact of Politics

While the poll finds bipartisan support for surveillance, the way the attitudes of Democrats and Republicans have shifted on the issue since President [Barack] Obama took office is once again evidence of the power of partisanship, rather than principle, in how voters see the world. For instance; the number of Democrats who say they think invading Iraq was the right choice has surged since Obama took office, and the number of Republican's who think it was a smart choice has plummeted.

The Pew poll found that in January 2006, 75 percent of Republicans found NSA surveillance programs "acceptable," while 61 percent of Democrats found them "unacceptable." In this June 2013 poll, Republican support dropped to 52 percent while Democrat support surged, to 64 percent now finding the surveillance programs acceptable.

While it's natural that Republicans would trust a Republican president more (and vice versa), expanded powers for the federal government don't expire at the end of each president's term. Still, even when it comes to fundamental questions about the trade-offs between privacy and security, a large portion of the electorate, like the politicians that lead them, don't look beyond the election cycle.

If You Are Sick of Surveillance, Safeguard Your Systems

C. Mitchell Shaw

C. Mitchell Shaw writes for The New American.

Thanks to the Snowden leaks, most people don't need to be convinced that data-mining by government agencies and irresponsible corporations is a real problem that threatens our liberties in the digital age. Fortunately, technology is an equal-opportunity tool. Remember that Snowden was able to keep himself and his communications from prying eyes while making not just one, but a series of revelations to journalists. The technologies he used are used by millions every day. They are easily available and largely free to download. Obviously, addressing all that needs to be done and how to do it is beyond the scope of any one article. This article will give you a good place to begin closing the door on those who would violate your online privacy, but it is up to you to learn more. Do an Internet search for the tools listed here, and you will find a trove of tutorials and YouTube videos to help you along the way. Using these tools may involve an uncomfortable learning curve, but the payoff is worth the effort.

Before addressing those technologies, a look at the nature of "Open-Source" software may be helpful. In simple terms, open-source software is licensed in such a way that its source code is available for anyone to view, audit, modify, and redistribute. Because the open-source community is so large and diverse, the likelihood of anything nefarious being hidden in the code is at or near zero. Another benefit of open-source software is that where vulnerabilities exist, they are more quickly discovered and patched as a community of thousands of people works to solve problems. That is why viruses, which are such a problem for Windows and, to a lesser degree, Mac, are unheard of for Linux.

Never put anything on the Internet that you would not want to see on the front page of your newspaper.

Linux is a great alternative to Windows for those seeking a more secure and liberty-friendly "Operating System." Because it is open-source, there are many different "flavors" (called distributions) available. Two of the most popular distributions are Ubuntu and Fedora. They can be downloaded for free from www.ubuntu.com and www.getfedora.org/. A fairly complete list of Linux distributions can be found at www.distrowatch.com.

While replacing Windows (or Mac) with Linux is the first step in securing your information, it is by no means sufficient in itself. Encrypting your hard drive should be the next step. Encryption turns the data on your hard drive into an unintelligible string of random characters until the correct password is entered. The protection offered by encrypting your hard drive is only as strong as your password, and though the encryption cannot be broken, a weak password can be broken within minutes using a brute force attack. A good password should be long and include uppercase and lowercase letters, numbers, and symbols. All encryption is not equal, as we now know that many encryption software companies have been pressured by the NSA to provide backdoors.

Because of this and the closed-source nature of many of these programs, you should only use open-source encryption. Luckily, most Linux distributions include encryption as part of the installation process.

Now that you have a secure operating system and an encrypted hard drive, it's time to look at the way you use the Internet. Never put anything on the Internet that you would not want to see on the front page of your newspaper. That applies not just to social media, but also to online backup and storage. As the recent hacking and subsequent leaking of intimate celebrity photos stored on Apple's iCloud service demonstrate, once it leaves your hands, it leaves your control. Regardless of the privacy agreements or security promises of these providers, *it is up to you to protect your data.* Besides, most social media and online backup and storage companies are more than willing to cooperate with government snooping. Dropbox recently announced Condoleezza Rice as the newest member of its board. It also keeps backups of files months after you delete them and even after you close your account. One way around this is to encrypt any file you backup or store online. A good tool for this is 7zip, which is available as a free download in most any Linux distribution. Another solution is to switch your online backups to a service that offers "zero knowledge" storage. One such service is SpiderOak, which offers encryption for which only you have the password. They cannot even see your data, not to mention allow anyone else, including government agencies, to see it. If required to turn your data over to a government agency, all they would be able to turn over would be the encrypted files and folders.

For the ultimate security while surfing the web, you want to be completely anonymous.

E-mail is a very insecure form of communication, as it can be intercepted quite easily. It is like sending a postcard through the mail. Anyone, anywhere along the way that intercepts it can read it. The ultimate solution is to encrypt your e-mail. Open-source GPG e-mail encryption is easily installed and is fairly easy to set up. Once you have it set up and get used to using it, the process is fairly transparent. Soon enough, you will forget you are even doing it, and your e-mail becomes inaccessible to snoopers, government and otherwise. Encourage your friends and family to begin encrypting their e-mails, as well. The more normal it becomes, the more people will do it and the more privacy we will all have.

As far as browsing the Internet, the bare minimum security would be to use a browser such as Firefox, which can be downloaded for free at www.mozilla.org. It is much more secure than Internet Explorer right out of the box, but there are some things you can do to make it even more secure. Download and install the HTTPS Everywhere plugin. This will force a secure connection on all sites that offer it. It is not perfect, but it is the same level of security/encryption used by banking websites. Disable third-party cookies and set up Flash to only run on sites you approve (a process called whitelisting). Flash is notoriously insecure and should only be used with caution.

For the ultimate security while surfing the web, you want to be completely anonymous. For that, there is Tor, which stands for The Onion Router. This service uses layers (like an onion) of security and encryption, routing your Internet traffic through a series of servers (called nodes) and creating a fake IP address at each point along the way. The result is that, when used properly, Tor creates real Internet anonymity. The websites you visit have no idea who you are and you cannot be tracked. This is the method Snowden used to contact *The Guardian* and leak the information on NSA spying. Tor is also available as part of a complete Linux distribution called T.A.I.L.S. (The Amnesic Incognito Live System), which runs only from a disc or usb drive. It leaves no trace of having been used and shuts down immediately if the disc or usb drive is removed.

Mobile devices are becoming easier to secure, as well. For many Android devices there are several after-market versions of Android available for those willing to root their devices.

Cyanogenmod is perhaps the most popular and certainly one of the most secure. It is free to download at www.cyano genmod.org. There are risks to rooting your device, however, and if it is not done correctly, it can make the device unusable. In the security settings of all Android devices there is the option of full encryption. For encrypted phone calls and texts on Android, there are applications available. TextSecure and RedPhone, both by Whisper Systems, are two of the best. Apple has claimed that new iPhones are able to be encrypted in a way that puts total control in the hands of the user. Since their software is closed-source, then believing this claim is a matter of trust, and Apple does not have the best record for being trustworthy. There are applications that claim to provide encrypted calls and texts for iPhone, as well, such as Babel, iCrypter, and CoverMe. Again, it's a matter of trust as to whether these tools are effective. There is one open-source solution for encrypted calls on iPhones. It is Signal, by Whisper Systems, the developers of TextSecure and RedPhone for Android.

There are many more tools available, but if you use those listed here properly, you will go a long way toward making yourself much harder for the NSA or irresponsible corporations to track and monitor. Unless you are a specific target, the tools outlined here are probably sufficient to shut the door in their faces and regain your privacy and security.

Total Surveillance Does Not Need to Be a Problem

Kevin Kelly

Kevin Kelly is the founding executive editor of Wired *magazine.*

I once worked with Steven Spielberg on the development of *Minority Report*, derived from the short story by Philip K. Dick featuring a future society that uses surveillance to arrest criminals before they commit a crime. I have to admit I thought Dick's idea of "pre-crime" to be unrealistic back then. I don't anymore.

The Inevitability of Surveillance

Most likely, 50 years from now ubiquitous monitoring and surveillance will be the norm. The internet is a tracking machine. It is engineered to track. We will ceaselessly self-track and *be* tracked by the greater network, corporations, and governments. Everything that can be measured is already tracked, and all that was previously unmeasureable is becoming quantified, digitized, and trackable.

We're expanding the data sphere to sci-fi levels and there's no stopping it. Too many of the benefits we covet derive from it. So our central choice now is whether this surveillance is a secret, one-way panopticon—or a mutual, transparent kind of "coveillance" that involves watching the watchers. The first option is hell, the second redeemable.

We can see both scenarios beginning today. We have the trade-secret algorithms of Google and Facebook on the one hand and the secret-obsessed NSA [National Security Agency] on the other. Networks require an immune system to remain healthy, and intense monitoring and occasional secrets are part of that hygiene to minimize the bad stuff. But in larger doses secrecy becomes toxic; more secrecy requires more secrets to manage and it sets up a debilitating auto-immune disease. This pathology is extremely difficult to stop, since by its own internal logic it must be stopped in secret.

The Remedy of Coveillance

The remedy for over-secrecy is to think in terms of coveillance, so that we make tracking and monitoring as symmetrical—and transparent—as possible. That way the monitoring can be regulated, mistakes appealed and corrected, specific boundaries set and enforced. A massively surveilled world is not a world I would design (or even desire), but massive surveillance is coming either way because that is the bias of digital technology and we might as well surveil well and civilly.

Encoding visible systems open to all eyes makes gaming them for secret ends more difficult.

In this version of surveillance—a transparent coveillance where everyone sees each other—a sense of entitlement can emerge: Every person has a human right to access, and benefit from, the data about themselves. The commercial giants running the networks have to spread the economic benefits of tracing people's behavior to the people themselves, simply to keep going. They will pay you to track yourself. Citizens film the cops, while the cops film the citizens. The business of monitoring (including those who monitor other monitors) will be a big business. The flow of money, too, is made more visible even as it gets more complex.

Much of this scenario will be made possible by the algorithmic regulation of information as pioneered by open source projects. For instance, while a system like Bitcoin makes anonymous bank accounts possible, it does so by transparently logging every transaction in its economy, therefore making all financial transactions public. PGP [Pretty Good Privacy] encryption relies on code that anyone can inspect, and therefore trust and verify. It generates "public privacy", so to speak.

Encoding visible systems open to all eyes makes gaming them for secret ends more difficult.

Every large system of governance—especially a digital society—is racked by an inherent tension between rigid fairness and flexible personalization. The cloud sees all: The cold justice of every tiny infraction by a citizen, whether knowingly or inadvertent, would be as inescapable as the logic of a software program. Yet we need the humanity of motive and context. One solution is to personalize justice to the context of that particular infraction. A symmetrically surveilled world needs a robust and flexible government—and transparency—to enforce adaptable fairness.

The self forged by previous centuries will no longer suffice. We are now remaking the self with technology.

The Human Impulse to Share

But if today's social media has taught us anything about ourselves as a species it is that the human impulse to share trumps the human impulse for privacy. So far, at every juncture that offers a technological choice between privacy or sharing, we've tilted, on average, towards more sharing, more disclosure. We shouldn't be surprised by this bias because transparency is truly ancient. For eons humans have lived in tribes and clans where every act was open and visible and there were no secrets. We evolved with constant co-monitoring. Contrary to our modern suspicions, there wouldn't be a backlash against a circular world where we constantly spy on each other because we lived like this for a million years, and—if truly equitable and symmetrical—it can feel comfortable.

41

Yet cities have "civilized" us with modern habits such as privacy. It is no coincidence that the glories of progress in the past 300 years parallel the emergence of the private self and challenges to the authority of society. Civilization is a mechanism to nudge us out of old habits. There would be no modernity without a triumphant self.

So while a world of total surveillance seems inevitable, we don't know if such a mode will nurture a strong sense of self, which is the engine of innovation and creativity—and thus all future progress. How would an individual maintain the boundaries of self when their every thought, utterance, and action is captured, archived, analyzed, and eventually anticipated by others?

The self forged by previous centuries will no longer suffice. We are now remaking the self with technology. We've broadened our circle of empathy, from clan to race, race to species, and soon beyond that. We've extended our bodies and minds with tools and hardware. We are now expanding our self by inhabiting virtual spaces, linking up to billions of other minds, and trillions of other mechanical intelligences. We are wider than we were, and as we offload our memories to infinite machines, deeper in some ways.

Amplified coveillance will shift society to become even more social; more importantly it will change how we define ourselves as humans.

CHAPTER 2

How Does Domestic Surveillance Affect Privacy and Security?

Public Perceptions of Privacy and Security in the Post-Snowden Era

Mary Madden

Mary Madden is a senior researcher at the Pew Research Center and an expert on social media use and online privacy management.

To better understand how the public thinks about privacy, a representative sample of 607 adults were asked an open-ended question in an online survey: "When you hear the word 'privacy,' what comes to mind for you?"[1] The responses that followed were striking in their variance, ranging from one-word entries to lengthier descriptions that touched on multiple concepts.

Once the responses were coded, a set of key words and themes emerged as the most frequently referenced and top-of-mind for the general public. Each of the top ten themes was referenced in at least 5% of the total responses. However, a full 22% of the responses referenced some other theme that was mentioned only a handful of times or was entirely unique.

A Large Segment of the Responses Associated Privacy with Concepts of *Security, Safety and Protection*

For many Americans, privacy is closely associated with references to security.[2] Even as "privacy" and "security" signal distinct sectors of technological development and legal protections, these concepts are often blurred and overlapping for the general public. Among all of the themes referenced in the open-ended responses to the online survey, security, safety and protection was the most frequently-referenced category; 14% of the responses used these phrases in some form. Respondents associated privacy with the "security of personal information" or as something that "must be protected." And among the most common one-word responses were simply the words "secure" and "security."

While online survey respondents most often used the term [privacy] in the context of "personal information," they also described privacy as personal in many other combinations.

In online focus groups, smaller groups of respondents from the survey were asked specifically about the way they think about privacy versus security online. In many cases, respondents viewed the terms as interchangeable:

Q: Is there any difference in the way you think about privacy and security online?

"I think it's pretty much the same."

"I see them as the same."

"Not to me, that is pretty much the same thing."

"Pretty much go hand [in] hand."

However, some participants viewed the concepts as more distinct, with security signaling issues around personal safety, financial matters and protection from external threats online:

"Privacy is keeping something from someone, security is having the confidence that things or you [are] going to be ok."

"In my mind, privacy deals more on the side of personal issues while security deals with financial issues."

*"Security to me means a firewall, a secure sight and a good fil-
ter on your computer. Privacy is more like photos, and personal info."*

Privacy Also Signals a Range of Things That Are Considered to Be *Personal*

As with the focus group discussions, a slightly smaller portion
of the survey responses (12%) used some variation of the
word, "personal." While online survey respondents most often
used the term in the context of "personal information," they
also described privacy as personal in many other combinations, such as: "my personal business," "personal life," "personal space," "personal stuff," "my personal solitude," and a
"personal right."

Many Respondents Associated Privacy with the Ability to Keep Some Things *Secret or Hidden*

About one in ten (11%) responses included the word "secret"
or some variation of things that are hidden. Respondents described privacy as: "keeping secret," "secret, private, for your
eyes only type of thing," or as things that are "protected, secret, concealed." Other responses suggested privacy as connected to having a "Hidden agenda" or things that are "secret,
undercover."

---

*Some 43% of adults have heard "a lot" about . . . gov-
ernment surveillance, and another 44% had heard "a
little."*

Other common themes that emerged from the open-ended
responses were clustered around privacy as:

- A set of rights, such as the "right to be let alone"
  (10%).

- Others "staying out of my business" (9%).

- Something people "don't have" or "doesn't exist" (9%).

- Associated with information and the ability to control and limit access to it (8%).

- Tied to the internet and technology (7%).

- Things people want to keep to themselves and no one else (7%).

- Associated with references to the National Security Agency (NSA) and Edward Snowden (5%).

Most Have Heard at Least a Little About Government Surveillance

Beyond specific references to government surveillance programs in the adults' associations with the word "privacy," almost all of the participants in our online panel said that they have heard at least something about "the government collecting information about telephone calls, emails, and other online communications as part of efforts to monitor terrorist activity." And those who have heard the most about the government disclosures are more privacy sensitive across an array of measures in the survey.[3]

Some 43% of adults have heard "a lot" about this government surveillance, and another 44% had heard "a little." Just 5% of adults in our panel said they had heard "nothing at all" about these programs.

Looking at demographics, we find that men were much more likely than women to say they have heard a lot about the NSA revelations (50% vs. 36%), and those ages 65 and older were more likely than younger age groups to have heard a lot (57% vs. 37% of those under age 50).[4] Adults with higher levels of education and household income were also more likely to report hearing a lot compared with those who have lower levels of education.

Those Who Have Heard "A Lot" About Government Surveillance Programs Are Also More Aware of Their Own Digital Footprints

A majority of adults say that they keep track of their digital footprints, but those who have a high level of awareness about government surveillance are more likely to say they search for information about themselves online. Overall, six in ten (62%) of those who participated in our online panel have ever used a search engine to look up their own name or see what information about them is on the internet.[5] Those who have heard a lot about government surveillance of communications are more likely to be self-searchers than those who have heard a little or nothing about it (71% vs 57%).[6]

Self-searching activity varies greatly across different groups, particularly by age, income, and household education. Adults under the age of 50 are far more likely to be "self-searchers" than those ages 50 and older, and adults with higher levels of household income and education stand out as especially likely to check up on their own digital footprints.

Close to eight in ten (80%) American adults "agree" or "strongly agree" that Americans should be concerned about the government's monitoring of phone calls and internet communications.

Few Feel It's a "Good Thing" for Society If People Believe They Are Being Watched Online

A majority of adults (62%) disagree with the statement "It is a good thing for society if people believe that someone is keeping an eye on the things that they do online," including 20% who "strongly disagree." Another 36% do agree that online surveillance is good for society, including the 7% who say they "strongly agree."

Attitudes about online surveillance vary greatly among different groups, particularly by age and education. For instance, adults ages 50 and older are generally less likely than younger adults to see online surveillance as beneficial. Those with lower levels of education are also more likely to be in favor of online surveillance, with 45% of those who have not attended college agreeing overall—compared with 33% of those with some college experience and 26% of college graduates.

Finally, adults who have heard more about government surveillance are more likely to think such oversight could have drawbacks: Just 23% of adults who have heard "a lot" about the NSA revelations think online surveillance is good for society, compared with 46% of those who have heard less about the NSA revelations.

Most Americans Agree That Citizens "Should Be Concerned" About the Government's Monitoring Programs

Close to eight in ten (80%) American adults "agree" or "strongly agree" that Americans should be concerned about the government's monitoring of phone calls and internet communications. Just 18% "disagree" or "strongly disagree" with that notion.

Overall, 40% "strongly agree" that American citizens should be concerned, while 39% "agree." Men are more likely than women to "strongly agree" that the monitoring programs are cause for concern (46% vs. 35%). However, there are no significant variations by age, income or education levels.

Those who have heard "a lot" about government surveillance programs are considerably more likely to hold strong views; 53% "strongly agree" that citizens should be concerned, compared with 33% of those who have heard only a little or nothing about the programs.

Endnotes

1. A full discussion of the sample is available at the end of this report.

2. This association is often communicated in various privacy policies directed at consumers with regard to data security. However, it is also worth noting here that a different concept of security may be evoked by the language of the Fourth Amendment, which emphasizes the "right of the people to be secure in their persons, houses, papers, and effects, against unreasonable searches and seizures." Specific references to the Fourth Amendment were coded separately, but some references to being "secure" could be overlapping in some cases.

3. Other recent surveys have found correlations between privacy-related awareness and concern. See, Chris Jay Hoofnagle and Jennifer M. Urban's discussion in "Alan Westin's Privacy Homo Economicus," available at: http://scholarship .law.berkeley.edu/cgi/viewcontent.cgi?article=3399&context=facpubs

4. Adults ages 65 and older are also more likely to keep up with news in general: http://www.people-press.org/2012/09/27/section-1-watching-reading-and -listening-to-the-news-3/

5. In May 2013, an RDD telephone survey of adults found that 56% of internet users had used a search engine to look up their own name and see what information is available about them online: http://www.pewresearch.org/fact-tank/2013 /09/27/majority-of-online-americansgoogle-themselves/

6. While self-searching activity is associated with several measures of increased privacy-related sensitivity throughout the survey, it is also worth noting that self-searching can be one way to link IP addresses to individual users.

How the NSA's Surveillance Procedures Threaten Americans' Privacy

American Civil Liberties Union

The American Civil Liberties Union is a national organization advocating for individual rights and liberties guaranteed by the US Constitution and US laws.

Newly released documents confirm what critics have long suspected—that the National Security Agency, a component of the Defense Department, is engaged in unconstitutional surveillance of Americans' communications, including their telephone calls and emails. The documents show that the NSA is conducting sweeping surveillance of Americans' international communications, that it is acquiring many purely domestic communications as well, and that the rules that supposedly protect Americans' privacy are weak and riddled with exceptions.

The FISA Amendment Act, signed into law by President Bush in 2008, expanded the government's authority to monitor Americans' electronic communications. Critics of the law feared the NSA would use the law to conduct broad surveillance of Americans' international communications and, in the process, capture an unknown quantity of purely domestic communications. Government officials contended that the law authorized surveillance of foreign nationals outside the United States—not of Americans—and that it included robust safeguards to protect Americans' privacy. Last year, in a successful effort to derail a constitutional challenge to the law, the Obama administration made these same claims to the U.S. Supreme Court.

Now *The Guardian* has published two previously secret documents that show how the FISA Amendments Act is being implemented. One document sets out the government's "targeting procedures"—the procedures it uses to determine whether it has the authority to acquire communications in the first place. The other sets out the government's "minimization procedures"—the procedures that govern the retention, analysis, and dissemination of the communications it acquires. Both documents—the "Procedures"—have apparently been endorsed by the Foreign Intelligence Surveillance Court, which oversees government surveillance in some national security cases.

Despite government officials' claims to the contrary, the NSA is building a growing database of Americans' international telephone calls and emails.

The Procedures are complex, but at least some of their flaws are clear.

1. The Procedures permit the NSA to monitor Americans' international communications in the course of surveillance targeted at foreigners abroad.

The NSA "is not listening to Americans' phone calls or monitoring their emails," the Chairman of the House Intelligence Committee recently said, and many other government officials, including the president himself, have made similar assurances. But these statements are not true. While the FISA Amendments Act authorizes the government to target foreigners abroad, not Americans, it permits the government to collect Americans' communications with those foreign targets. Indeed, in advocating for the Act, government officials made clear that these "one-end-domestic" communications were the ones of most interest to them. The Procedures contemplate not only that the NSA will acquire Americans' international communications but that it will retain them and possibly disseminate them to other U.S. government agencies and foreign governments. Americans' communications that contain "foreign intelligence information" or evidence of a crime can be retained forever, and even communications that don't can be retained for as long as five years. Despite government officials' claims to the contrary, the NSA is building a growing database of Americans' international telephone calls and emails.

2. The Procedures allow the surveillance of Americans by failing to ensure that the NSA's surveillance targets are in fact foreigners outside the United States.

The Act is predicated on the theory that foreigners abroad have no right to privacy—or, at any rate, no right that the United States should respect. Because they have no right to privacy, the U.S. government sees no bar to the collection of their communications, including their communications with Americans. But even if one accepts the government's premise, the Procedures fail to ensure that the NSA's surveillance targets are *in fact* foreigners outside the United States. This is because the Procedures permit the NSA to *presume* that prospective surveillance targets are foreigners outside the United States absent specific information to the contrary—and to presume therefore that they are fair game for warrantless surveillance.

3. The Procedures permit the government to conduct surveillance that has no real connection to the government's foreign intelligence interests.

However the NSA does it, the result is the same: millions of communications may be swept up, Americans' international communications among them.

One of the fundamental problems with the Act is that it permits the government to conduct surveillance without probable cause or individualized suspicion. It permits the government to monitor people who aren't even thought to be doing anything wrong, and to do so without particularized warrants or meaningful review by impartial judges. Government officials have placed heavy emphasis on the fact that the Act allows the government to conduct surveillance only if one of its purposes is to gather "foreign intelligence information." That term, though, is defined very broadly to include not only information about terrorism but also information about intelligence activities, the national defense, and even "the foreign affairs of the United States." The Procedures weaken the limitation further. Among the things the NSA examines to determine whether a particular email address or phone number will be used to exchange foreign intelligence information is whether it has been used in the past to communicate with foreigners. Another is whether it is listed in a foreigner's address book. In other words, the NSA seems to equate a propensity to communicate with foreigners with a propensity to communicate foreign intelligence information. The effect is to bring virtually every international communication within the reach of the NSA's surveillance.

4. The Procedures permit the NSA to collect international communications, including Americans' international communications, in bulk.

On its face, the Act permits the NSA to conduct dragnet surveillance, not just surveillance of specific individuals. Officials who advocated for the Act made clear that this was one of its principal purposes, and unsurprisingly, the Procedures give effect to that design. While they require the government to identify a "target" outside the country, once the target has been identified the Procedures permit the NSA to sweep up the communications of any foreigner who may be communicating "about" the target. The Procedures contemplate that the NSA will do this by "employ[ing] an Internet Protocol filter to ensure that the person from whom it seeks to obtain foreign intelligence information is located overseas," by "target[ing] Internet links that terminate in a foreign country," or by identifying "the country code of the telephone number." However the NSA does it, the result is the same: millions of communications may be swept up, Americans' international communications among them.

5. The Procedures allow the NSA to retain even purely domestic communications.

Given the permissive standards the NSA uses to determine whether prospective surveillance targets are foreigners abroad, errors are inevitable. Some of the communications the NSA collects under the Act, then, will be purely domestic. (Notably, a 2009 *New York Times* article discusses an episode in which the NSA used the Act to engage in "significant and systemic" overcollection of such domestic communications.) The Act should require the NSA to purge these communications from its databases, but it does not. The Procedures allow the government to keep and analyze even purely domestic communications if they contain significant foreign intelligence information, evidence of a crime, or encrypted information. Again, foreign intelligence information is defined exceedingly broadly. The result is that the NSA is steadily building a database of Americans' purely domestic calls and emails.

The Procedures' reference to "Home Location Registers" ... suggests that the NSA also collects some form of location information about millions of Americans' cellphones.

---

6. The Procedures allow the government to collect and retain communications protected by the attorney-client privilege.

The Procedures expressly contemplate that the NSA will collect attorney-client communications. In general, these communications receive no special protection—they can be acquired, retained, and disseminated like any other. Thus, if the NSA acquires the communications of lawyers representing individuals who have been charged before the military commissions at Guantanamo, nothing in the Procedures would seem to prohibit the NSA from sharing the communications with military prosecutors. The Procedures include a more restrictive rule for communications between attorneys and their clients who have been criminally indicted in the United States— the NSA may not share these communications with prosecutors. Even those communications, however, may be retained to the extent that they include foreign intelligence information.

7. The Procedures contemplate that the NSA will maintain "knowledge databases" containing sensitive information about Americans.

To determine whether a target is a foreigner abroad, the Procedures contemplate that the NSA will consult various NSA databases containing information collected by it and other agencies through signals intelligence, human intelligence, law enforcement, and other means. These databases— referred to as "NSA content repositories" and "knowledge databases"—apparently house internet data, including metadata that reveals online activities, as well as telephone numbers and email addresses that the agency has reason to believe are being used by U.S. persons. The Procedures' reference to "Home Location Registers," which receive updates whenever a phone "moves into a new service area," suggests that the NSA also collects some form of location information about millions of Americans' cellphones. The Procedures do not say what limits apply to these databases or what safeguards, if any, are in place to protect Americans' constitutional rights.

8. The Procedures allow the NSA to retain encrypted communications indefinitely.

The Procedures permit the NSA to retain, forever, all communications—even purely domestic ones—that are encrypted. The use of encryption to protect data is a routine and sometimes legally required practice by financial organizations, health care providers, and real-time communications services (like Skype and Apple's FaceTime). Accordingly, the Procedures permit the NSA to retain huge volumes of Americans' most sensitive information.

Internet Surveillance Is a Necessary Part of National Security

Daniel J. Gallington

Daniel J. Gallington is the senior policy and program adviser at the George C. Marshall Institute.

Consider the assumptions and conclusions about Internet privacy in the following recent quote from a Fox News article:

> Bruce Schneier, a security expert who worked with the *Guardian* to reveal the NSA's secrets, said Thursday [September 5, 2013] that the U.S. government had "betrayed the Internet."

> "By subverting the Internet at every level to make it a vast, multi-layered and robust surveillance platform, the NSA has undermined a fundamental social contract," Schneier wrote in an essay for the British paper.

> "We can no longer trust them to be ethical Internet stewards. This is not the Internet the world needs, or the Internet its creators envisioned. We need to take it back."

> The American Civil Liberties Union [ACLU] joined Schneier in criticizing the spy agency. Christopher Soghoian, principal technologist of the ACLU's Speech, Privacy and Technology Project, said late Thursday that the agency's alleged campaign against encryption "is making the Internet less secure" and exposing Web users to "criminal hacking, foreign espionage, and unlawful surveillance."

Daniel J. Gallington, "The Case for Internet Surveillance," *U.S. News & World Report*, September 18, 2013. © Wright's Media. All Rights Reserved. Reproduced by permission.

The thrust of these comments is that the Internet should be—somehow—immune from any government surveillance of any kind and for any reason. This idea reminds me of a conversation I had with my 90-year-old mom several years ago, when she suggested the same thing. So, I asked her, "OK mom, but what about spies, terrorists and kidnappers?" She thought (for just a second) and said, "Well, those kind of people . . . sure," as if I should have known that she meant to exclude "those kind of people."

In most of the rest of the world, there is content surveillance and monitoring of Internet based traffic by one or more government intelligence or law enforcement agencies.

Privacy in Communication

These same arguments were made about the telephone many years ago, especially when organized crime started using it to conduct its "business." And then, just like the terrorist threat today, it "cost us" a bit of our privacy to be able to track the Mafia with wiretaps. In fact, had it not been for wiretaps, the war against organized crime would have been lost decades ago.

In addition, we Americans need to get that we are truly unique in the world because of our traditional insistence on private sector dominance in our telecommunications industry—this continues as we have gone wireless and concentrated on Internet based communications.

More specifically, in most other parts of the world—democratic or not—the communications infrastructures are mostly government owned or operated, similar to (or even part of) the post office. So also, in most of the rest of the world, there is content surveillance and monitoring of Internet based traffic by one or more government intelligence or law enforcement agencies—and usually without any threshold showing or requirement for probable cause or reasonable belief to look at the substance of the communication. Similarly: Check into any hotel in Europe, and you must show your passport or your required identity card, and your personal data goes directly to the national police or internal security service for whatever checks on you they want to make.

And, it goes without saying that everywhere in the undemocratic world, e.g., China, everyone is watched all the time, including all Internet activity, because all dissent is a threat to the regime in power, and that's simply how they stay in power and have always stayed in power. In the past they did it with networks of spies and informants, and now with total Internet supervision.

Much to the concern of despots everywhere, however, is that today's Internet is evolving—at least conceptually—to everyone having or having access to their own shortwave-like capability to be able to talk to anybody anywhere in the world.

Questions About Internet Privacy

So, two key policy questions emerge from this discussion and the technical realities of today's Internet:

- First, do all of us, including the spies, terrorists and kidnappers among us, have a reasonable expectation of privacy when we use the Internet today? And to what extent, if any, have the various democratic governments betrayed the modern day realities of the Internet by their various degrees of monitoring?

- Second, what effect—if any—on the expectation of privacy should efforts to encrypt Internet communications have? In other words, when someone encrypts their Internet communications, are they somehow entitled to more privacy or does it make the Internet less secure because of the government's possible need to decrypt it, for one reason or another, good or bad. Even more fundamental perhaps—and not intended to be silly—should spies, terrorists and kidnappers be able to encrypt their communications with the expectation of privacy?

Frankly, such assertions are not helpful in the current debate, primarily because they don't address the reasons and thresholds for surveillances, nor the oversight of the processes for it in our democracy.

It would seem that, in turn, the key to these questions (and also the key to whether our government has been and is acting responsibly) is this more fundamental question: How do we determine whether someone's or something's Internet communications are related to espionage, terrorism or criminal activity—the assumption here being that if they are, then our government should know about it and be able to watch them to keep us safe.

It seems reasonable to conclude that: 1) The expectation of Internet privacy does not, should not—never has and never should—extend to spies, terrorists and criminals; 2) Our government should be monitoring the communications of these people, whether they are encrypted or not (and perhaps especially if they are); and 3) Our main focus, therefore, should be on how, who and on what basis (or threshold) a determination is made to look at a particular Internet communication or category of communications, and how this determination is monitored and by who.

Now, we're getting somewhere, and I would invite my colleague Mr. Schneier and the ACLU (for whom I have the utmost respect) to comment more specifically on this aspect of the equation, rather than merely asserting that the government has somehow "betrayed," "subverted" or "undermined" the Internet. Frankly, such assertions are not helpful in the current debate, primarily because they don't address the reasons and thresholds for surveillances, nor the oversight of the processes for it in our democracy.

The Parameters of Justified Surveillance

Let's float some ideas for such a rational and objective discussion:

First, if we knew, based on reliable information or sources—a human source for example—that Internet user X was in fact engaged in espionage, terrorism or criminal activity, it seems clear that our system should enable intrusive surveillance of X's Internet usage, just as it would X's telephone. Also, it would seem reasonable to also look at whom X was communicating with, if only to see if the communications were routine—e.g., to order a pizza—or if they were to someone else engaged in espionage, terrorism or criminal activity or were somehow related to those activities.

Second, assuming it were technically possible to somehow sort through huge amounts of Internet traffic, by using key words or other kinds of data in some kind of search engine, and if there were several layers of review, including human review, in such a process, could it then be reasonable to selectively look at the content of the traffic, provided such was also 1) approved by a judge or a senior official, and 2) was allowed for only a limited period of time, and 3) was subject to periodic review? This kind of examination may not necessarily require the identity of the communicators, until and unless such was approved by an additional/similar process that required a specific approval.

Would such an approach to looking at Internet traffic for spies, terrorists and criminals be 1) reasonable 2) constitutional, and could it be established by public law and implemented by executive order and regulation, provided the Congress was kept in the loop with regular oversight reporting?

If the answer to these questions continues to be yes—and it most likely is—then the recent public debate brought on by Edward Snowden's disclosures is far more mundane, and far less sensational than the media would perhaps like it to be. Also in that case, the real issue set boils down to the following set of key questions, best answered by our Congress—specifically the Intelligence committees working with some other key committees—after a searching inquiry and a series of hearings, as many of them open as possible.

- Were the established and relevant laws, regulations and procedures complied with?

- Are the established laws, regulations and procedures up to date for current Internet and other technologies?

- Is there reason to add new laws, regulations and procedures?

- Is there a continued requirement—based on public safety—to be able to do intrusive surveillance, including Internet surveillance, against spies, terrorists or criminals?

In sum, the idea that we have somehow "betrayed" or "subverted" the Internet (or the telephone for that matter) is—as my mom also used to say—"just plain silly." Such kinds of inaccurate statements are emotional and intended mostly for an audience with preconceived opinions or that hasn't thought very hard about the dangerous consequences of an Internet totally immune from surveillance. In fact, it seems time for far less sensationalism—primarily by the media—and far more objectivity. In the final analysis, my mom probably had it right: "Those kind of people, sure."

A Balance Can Be Struck Between Privacy and Security

Monte Frenkel

Monte Frenkel is a legal fellow at the Brennan Center for Justice and a law student at New York University School of Law.

Thirty-eight years before Edward Snowden's leaks, the NSA [National Security Agency] was embroiled in its first real scandal over secret surveillance. Then NSA director, Lt. General Lew Allen, was the first director in the agency's history to publicly testify before Congress. A quick review of the circumstances surrounding his historic testimony reminds us that it is naïve to think that a permanent, universally acceptable balance between privacy and security can ever be struck, especially in a world of rapid technological change. But it also reminds us that abuses, even severe ones, can be met by serious investigation and broad debate—and that reforms, even if temporary, are possible.

The Church Committee

At the time of Allen's testimony in 1975, the Church Committee—a group of Senators charged with investigating intelligence and federal law enforcement abuses—was examining a pair of linked NSA operations: Project SHAMROCK and Project MINARET. SHAMROCK actually predated the NSA, originating with World War II Army censors, who had access to the nation's correspondence through their presence in telegraph offices. With the war ending, top administration officials convinced the major private telegraph operators, then the titans that stood astride international communication, to provide copies of all messages leaving the United States. The program collected huge numbers of messages, though the NSA purported to separate messages of "foreign intelligence value" from the rest, and to avoid collecting communications that involved only U.S. citizens.

The secretive FISA court was an effort to balance the executive's perceived need for information and secrecy with the strictures of the law and the Constitution.

But technology and customer requirements soon changed. In the 1960s, the telegraph companies handing over the messages, for the most part, stopped providing paper records for the NSA to copy onto microfilm and instead began allowing the NSA to copy magnetic tapes directly. This made it much easier not just to screen the messages based on broad criteria, but to search the messages themselves.

Starting in 1967, the executive branch, facing levels of domestic unrest not seen in decades, started asking the NSA to search these outgoing messages for information on U.S. citizens and domestic groups. The use of SHAMROCK information to monitor a list of domestic entities became known as MINARET. Through MINARET, the government spied not only on suspected drug runners, but also on "extremist" persons, anti-war protestors, and other targets of interest, resulting in more than 1,600 U.S citizens being tracked. As Sen. Frank Church (D-Idaho), chairman of the Church Committee, noted, many people who were "wholly inappropriate for . . . surveillance" ended up having their mail opened and private messages read.

And so General Allen came before the Church Committee to defend such agency actions. The call and response between Allen and his supporters in Congress is particularly familiar to our contemporary ears. In his opening statement, Allen asserted that the agency had "strict procedures to [e]nsure immediate and, where possible, automatic rejection of inappropriate messages ... [examining only] messages which meet specified conditions and requirements for foreign intelligence." Sen. John Tower (R-Texas) noted that the NSA was appropriately employing advance "computer age" technology and that "the people's right to know must of necessity be subordinated to the people's right to be secure."

The FISA Court

Nonetheless, Congress took action to curb the NSA's activities. The FISA [Foreign Intelligence Surveillance Act] court was created by Congress in 1978 largely as a reaction to MINARET and SHAMROCK. The secretive FISA court was an effort to balance the executive's perceived need for information and secrecy with the strictures of the law and the Constitution. Today, before conducting "electronic surveillance anywhere in the United States" for foreign intelligence purposes, executive agencies must get FISA court approval.

The balance we seek to strike today is the same one that has stymied policymakers for decades.

Today, PRISM and dragnet metadata collection under Section 215 of the Patriot Act, controversial as these programs are, stand as a testament to the tangible role the FISA court plays in monitoring the intelligence community. In contrast to SHAMROCK, these programs involve at least some regular oversight from entities outside the NSA. The government also disclaims any intentional collection of purely domestic communications related to these programs, even if it does collect domestic metadata. FISA court oversight is far from perfect, but it has certainly changed the landscape of foreign intelligence surveillance.

In other ways, though, the problem remains the same. As in the 1970s, today's programs matured behind a shroud of classification, coming to public attention in spite of attempts at secrecy. Then, as now, the sheer scale of the collection is mind boggling, and the efforts to protect U.S. citizens from undue invasions of their privacy are too secretive and too easily circumvented to justify reliance on the executive's good intentions.

Also eerily similar is the debate over just what is legal. At a Church Committee hearing, Sen. Walter Mondale (D-Minn.), after questioning an NSA official on MINARET and SHAMROCK's justifications, exclaimed, "He still thinks they're legal!"—a shout that echoes today as we once again consider the proper role of government surveillance in our democracy.

It is tempting to think that advancing technology has launched us into a brave new world of surveillance in which history can provide no guidance. But that is rarely the case, and it is not so here. The balance we seek to strike today is the same one that has stymied policymakers for decades. And the lesson is clear: surveillance authorities are prone to abuse—but amenable to reform.

After Charlie Hebdo Massacre, We Must Ratchet Up Policing and Intelligence-Gathering to Catch Every Possible Terrorist

Michael Sheehan

Michael Sheehan is assistant secretary of defense for Special Operations and Low-Intensity Conflict in the US Department of Defense.

The horrific terrorist attack in Paris underscores the importance of retaining our focus on preventing attacks here in the United States. This requires a layered, proactive, aggressive and relentless strategy that identifies the attacker before he launches an attack.

A purely defensive strategy of protecting our critical infrastructure, which is what some people would have us settle for, will not be sufficient in our open society.

The search for terrorists at home begins overseas, as they travel to and from the United States, and continues within the homeland.

Overseas, American partnership with local intelligence services have been effective since 9/11. Our CIA station chiefs around the world have been charged with getting intelligence from our partners.

The key to our success here is best understood by the maxim of my partner at NYPD and 35-year career intelligence officer, David Cohen. Cohen says there is no such thing as "intelligence sharing"—there is only "intelligence trading." Real secrets are traded among serious collectors of intelligence. And our ability to get good actionable intelligence from our partners depends on our ability to provide them with the same.

It is no coincidence that the Charlie Hebdo terrorists had been on the U.S. no-fly list for years.

In my experience, one of the most effective tools we have in this regard is our enormous NSA signals-intelligence collection program. NSA, that recently maligned agency, is one of our nation's true jewels. Its enormous collection platforms enable us to share vital intelligence with our partners—who are happy to return the favor, often intelligence collected by their human sources.

NSA also passes critical intelligence data collected abroad through the CIA to the FBI's Joint Terrorist Task Forces around the country. This enables the FBI to focus its investigations on people identified with connections to terrorist organizations abroad.

This intelligence, in conjunction with human intelligence collected by CIA unilaterally or through its partnership with local intelligence services, informs the no-travel lists that are so crucial to protecting our shores from traveling terrorists. Indeed, it is no coincidence that the Charlie Hebdo terrorists had been on the U.S. no-fly list for years.

But these lists are not enough. Aggressive intelligence is required at our border—and within our neighborhoods. At the border, we must increase the use of secondary inspections in our airports and other border crossings. These secondary inspections pull people from security lines and enable trained personnel to conduct brief interviews in separate rooms.

It is hard to understate the value of these inspections. "Secondaries" serve multiple purposes. They are a deterrent to terrorists contemplating travel to the U.S., who will never know when they get yanked out a line and questioned.

In addition, secondary inspections are a rich source of future informants—the key to unraveling cells within the United States.

Aggressive, non-politically correct secondary inspections will, in fact, target young men between 18 and 30 years old traveling from certain countries. Indeed this is a form of profiling.

But without profiling travelers it is virtually impossible to get real results. There are simply too many travelers, and not enough inspectors to pick randomly and hope for the best.

Inside the United States, counterterrorism investigations conducted by the FBI terrorism task forces and NYPD intelligence are the most effective way to catch a terrorist before he attacks. Random car stops or other generic police tactics will not get it done. We need targeted investigations that are managed by the laws of the land and limited by the Patriot Act of 2001.

Unfortunately, it is only the NYPD that conducts counterterrorism investigations outside of the FBI task forces—and it gets plenty of grief from the federal government for doing so.

The two biggest obstacles to finding terrorists within our midst are complacency and political correctness.

Other local police forces should expand their counterterrorism activities, coordinated with the FBI to ensure all potential leads and suspects are properly investigated and surveilled if necessary.

It is unconscionable that the two Chechen Boston marathon bombers were not under surveillance based on the threat warnings received by the Russian government. Cops know how to do this; it is not that different from running counternarcotics investigations.

The two biggest obstacles to finding terrorists within our midst are complacency and political correctness. We must overcome both of these and conduct legal, thorough and aggressive investigations at our border and within our cities.

Fortunately, our terrorist adversaries make many mistakes. If we are alert and on the job, we will identify these mistakes and intercept the vast majority of attacks before they happen. There is no guarantee of course that we will catch every would-be murderer. But we know how to increase the odds in our favor. We need to direct our law enforcement and intelligence services to get to it. And support them when they conduct their jobs to protect us.

Bulk Surveillance Programs Are Ineffective in Catching Terrorists

Peter Bergen et al.

Along with Peter Bergen, David Sterman, Emily Schneider, and Bailey Cahall contributed to the following viewpoint. Bergen is the director of the National Security Program at the New America Foundation, where Sterman and Schneider are research assistants and Cahall is a research associate.

On June 5, 2013, the *Guardian* broke the first story in what would become a flood of revelations regarding the extent and nature of the NSA's [National Security Agency's] surveillance programs. Facing an uproar over the threat such programs posed to privacy, the [Barack] Obama administration scrambled to defend them as legal and essential to U.S. national security and counterterrorism. Two weeks after the first leaks by former NSA contractor Edward Snowden were published, President Obama defended the NSA surveillance programs during a visit to Berlin, saying: "We know of at least 50 threats that have been averted because of this information not just in the United States, but, in some cases, threats here in Germany. So lives have been saved." Gen. Keith Alexander, the director of the NSA, testified before Congress that: "the information gathered from these programs provided the U.S. government with critical leads to help prevent over 50 potential terrorist events in more than 20 countries around the world." Rep. Mike Rogers (R-Mich.), chairman of the House Permanent Select Committee on Intelligence, said on the

Peter Bergen, David Sterman, Emily Schneider, and Bailey Cahall, "Do NSA's Bulk Surveillance Programs Stop Terrorists?," New America Foundation, January 13, 2014, pp. 1–3. © New America Foundation. All Rights Reserved. Reproduced by permission.

House floor in July that "54 times [the NSA programs] stopped and thwarted terrorist attacks both here and in Europe—saving real lives."

A careful review of three of the key terrorism cases the government has cited to defend NSA bulk surveillance programs reveals that government officials have exaggerated the role of the NSA in [these] cases.

The Efficacy of Surveillance

However, our review of the government's claims about the role that NSA "bulk" surveillance of phone and email communications records has had in keeping the United States safe from terrorism shows that these claims are overblown and even misleading. An in-depth analysis of 225 individuals recruited by al-Qaeda or a like-minded group or inspired by al-Qaeda's ideology, and charged in the United States with an act of terrorism since 9/11, demonstrates that traditional investigative methods, such as the use of informants, tips from local communities, and targeted intelligence operations, provided the initial impetus for investigations in the majority of cases, while the contribution of NSA's bulk surveillance programs to these cases was minimal. Indeed, the controversial bulk collection of American telephone metadata, which includes the telephone numbers that originate and receive calls, as well as the time and date of those calls but not their content, under Section 215 of the USA PATRIOT Act, appears to have played an identifiable role in, at most, 1.8 percent of these cases. NSA programs involving the surveillance of non-U.S. persons outside of the United States under Section 702 of the FISA [Foreign Intelligence Surveillance Act] Amendments Act played a role in 4.4 percent of the terrorism cases we examined, and NSA surveillance under an unidentified authority played a role in 1.3 percent of the cases we examined. Regular FISA warrants not issued in connection with Section 215 or Section

702, which are the traditional means for investigating foreign persons, were used in at least 48 (21 percent) of the cases we looked at, although it's unclear whether these warrants played an initiating role or were used at a later point in the investigation.

The overall problem for U.S. counterterrorism officials is not that they need vaster amounts of information from the bulk surveillance programs, but that they don't sufficiently understand or widely share the information they already possess.

Surveillance of American phone metadata has had no discernible impact on preventing acts of terrorism and only the most marginal of impacts on preventing terrorist-related activity, such as fundraising for a terrorist group. Furthermore, our examination of the role of the database of U.S. citizens' telephone metadata in the single plot the government uses to justify the importance of the program—that of Basaaly Moalin, a San Diego cabdriver who in 2007 and 2008 provided $8,500 to al-Shabaab, al-Qaeda's affiliate in Somalia—calls into question the necessity of the Section 215 bulk collection program. According to the government, the database of American phone metadata allows intelligence authorities to quickly circumvent the traditional burden of proof associated with criminal warrants, thus allowing them to "connect the dots" faster and prevent future 9/11-scale attacks. Yet in the Moalin case, after using the NSA's phone database to link a number in Somalia to Moalin, the FBI [Federal Bureau of Investigation] waited two months to begin an investigation and wiretap his phone. Although it's unclear why there was a delay between the NSA tip and the FBI wiretapping, court documents show there was a two-month period in which the FBI was not monitoring Moalin's calls, despite official statements that the bureau had Moalin's phone number and had identified him.

This undercuts the government's theory that the database of Americans' telephone metadata is necessary to expedite the investigative process, since it clearly didn't expedite the process in the single case the government uses to extol its virtues.

Additionally, a careful review of three of the key terrorism cases the government has cited to defend NSA bulk surveillance programs reveals that government officials have exaggerated the role of the NSA in the cases against David Coleman Headley and Najibullah Zazi, and the significance of the threat posed by a notional plot to bomb the New York Stock Exchange.

The Impact on Counterterrorism

In 28 percent of the cases we reviewed, court records and public reporting do not identify which specific methods initiated the investigation. These cases, involving 62 individuals, may have been initiated by an undercover informant, an undercover officer, a family member tip, other traditional law enforcement methods, CIA- or FBI-generated intelligence, NSA surveillance of some kind, or any number of other methods. In 23 of these 62 cases (37 percent), an informant was used. However, we were unable to determine whether the informant initiated the investigation or was used after the investigation was initiated as a result of the use of some other investigative means. Some of these cases may also be too recent to have developed a public record large enough to identify which investigative tools were used.

We have also identified three additional plots that the government has not publicly claimed as NSA successes, but in which court records and public reporting suggest the NSA had a role. However, it is not clear whether any of those three cases involved bulk surveillance programs.

Finally, the overall problem for U.S. counterterrorism officials is not that they need vaster amounts of information from the bulk surveillance programs, but that they don't sufficiently understand or widely share the information they already possess that was derived from conventional law enforcement and intelligence techniques. This was true for two of the 9/11 hijackers who were known to be in the United States before the attacks on New York and Washington, as well as with the case of Chicago resident David Coleman Headley, who helped plan the 2008 terrorist attacks in Mumbai, and it is the unfortunate pattern we have also seen in several other significant terrorism cases.

CHAPTER 3

Is Domestic Surveillance Constitutional?

Overview: Legislation Authorizing Government Surveillance

Edward C. Liu

Edward C. Liu is a legislative attorney for Congressional Research Service, which provides policy and legal analysis to the US Congress.

Reauthorizations of expiring provisions of the Foreign Intelligence Surveillance Act (FISA) have been an annual occurrence in Congress since 2009. Prior to 2012, the legislative debate and reauthorizations largely dealt with three amendments to FISA that are commonly linked to the Uniting and Strengthening America by Providing Appropriate Tools Required to Intercept and Obstruct Terrorism Act of 2001 (USA PATRIOT Act). Most recently, in 2011, these three provisions were extended until June 1, 2015. . . .

FISA and Other Laws Governing Surveillance

The Foreign Intelligence Surveillance Act (FISA) provides a statutory framework by which government agencies may, when gathering foreign intelligence information, obtain authorization to conduct wiretapping or physical searches, utilize pen registers and trap and trace devices, or access specified business records and other tangible things. Authorization for such activities is typically obtained via a court order from the Foreign Intelligence Surveillance Court (FISC), a specialized court

Edward C. Liu, "Reauthorization of the FISA Amendments Act," *CRS Report for Congress*, R42725, Congressional Research Service, April 8, 2013, pp. 1–4. © Congressional Research Service. All Rights Reserved. Reproduced by permission.

created by FISA to act as a neutral judicial decision maker in the context of activities authorized by the statute.

In some circumstances, the use of surveillance activities for foreign intelligence purposes might fall within the scope of the activities prohibited by [the Electronic Communications Privacy Act].

Title VII, added by the FISA Amendments Act of 2008, provides additional procedures for the acquisition of foreign intelligence information regarding persons who are believed to be outside of the United States. These provisions affect both U.S. persons as well as other non-U.S. persons. Specifically, the FISA Amendments Act added

- a new procedure for targeting non-U.S. persons abroad without individualized court orders;

- a new requirement to obtain an individualized court order when targeting U.S. persons abroad; and

- new procedures that can be used to obtain court orders authorizing the targeting of U.S. persons abroad for electronic surveillance, the acquisition of stored communications, and other means of acquiring foreign intelligence information.

FISA is just one of several federal laws that govern the use of electronic surveillance for legitimate investigative purposes. The principal others are the Electronic Communications Privacy Act (ECPA), Executive Order 12333, and the Fourth Amendment. . . .

The Electronic Communications Privacy Act (ECPA)

ECPA provides three sets of general prohibitions accompanied by judicially supervised exceptions to facilitate law enforcement investigations. The prohibitions address (1) the interception of wire, oral, or electronic communications (wiretapping); (2) access to the content of stored electronic communications and to communications transaction records; and (3) the use of trap and trace devices and pen registers (essentially in-and-out secret "caller id" devices).

In some circumstances, the use of surveillance activities for foreign intelligence purposes might fall within the scope of the activities prohibited by ECPA. There are two exceptions to ECPA's general prohibitions that address this situation.

First, if the activity in question falls within the definition of electronic surveillance under FISA, then it may be conducted if the government complies with FISA's procedures. For example, the interception of a domestic telephone call is the type of activity that would generally be prohibited by ECPA. It would also qualify as electronic surveillance under FISA. Therefore, if the government obtained a court order from the FISC authorizing the interception of that call, it would be a lawful surveillance activity notwithstanding the general prohibition against wiretapping found in ECPA.

The Fourth Amendment to the U.S. Constitution protects against "unreasonable searches and seizures."

Second, if the activity in question is not electronic surveillance, as that term is defined in FISA, but involves the acquisition of foreign intelligence information from international or foreign communications, then it is not subject to ECPA. For example, the interception of an international telephone call would not be considered electronic surveillance for purposes of FISA if the target were the person on the non-domestic end of the conversation and the acquisition would not occur on United States soil. So long as the purpose of that acquisition was to acquire foreign intelligence information, then it would not be subject to the general prohibitions in ECPA.

Although both exceptions result in the non-application of ECPA, they differ in one important aspect that is particularly relevant to understanding the changes wrought by Title VII of FISA. Both ECPA and FISA provide that the two statutes constitute the exclusive means of conducting electronic surveillance, as defined in FISA. As a result, using the procedures under FISA is compulsory for those activities that qualify as electronic surveillance but cannot be accomplished by, and are exempt from, ECPA. In contrast, prior to the FISA Amendments Act, FISA's procedures were generally never needed for wiretapping activities that did not qualify as electronic surveillance, and which were also exempt from ECPA because they involved international or foreign communications. However, ... the recently added § 704 of FISA does make FISA's procedures compulsory when the target of such surveillance is a United States person. Those activities that remain beyond the scope of either ECPA or FISA are governed by Executive Order 12333 and the Fourth Amendment, discussed in the next two sections.

Executive Order 12333 and the Fourth Amendment

Section 2.5 of Executive Order 12333, as amended, delegates to the Attorney General the power to approve the use of any technique for intelligence purposes within the United States or against a U.S. person abroad. If a warrant would be required for law enforcement purposes, the executive order requires the Attorney General to determine in each case that there is probable cause to believe that the technique is directed against a foreign power or an agent of a foreign power. The authority delegated by Executive Order 12333 must be exercised in accordance with FISA, but also extends to activities beyond FISA's reach.

The Fourth Amendment to the U.S. Constitution protects against "unreasonable searches and seizures." In domestic criminal law investigations, it generally requires law enforcement officers to obtain a court-issued warrant before conducting a search. When the warrant requirement does not apply, government activity is generally subject to a "reasonableness" test under the Fourth Amendment.

The extent to which the warrant requirement applies to the government's collection of foreign intelligence is unclear. In a 1972 case, the Supreme Court invalidated warrantless electronic surveillance of domestic organizations on Fourth Amendment grounds, despite the government's assertion of a national security rationale. However, it indicated that its conclusion might be different in a future case involving the electronic surveillance of foreign powers or their agents, within or outside the United States. In a 2002 case, the Foreign Intelligence Surveillance Court of Review upheld FISA, as amended by the USA PATRIOT Act, against a Fourth Amendment challenge. The court assumed, without deciding the question, that FISA court orders do not constitute warrants for purposes of the Fourth Amendment analysis. Relying on a general reasonableness analysis, it nonetheless upheld such orders, emphasizing both the privacy protections in the statutory framework and the governmental interest in preventing national security threats.

NSA Surveillance in Perspective

Roger Pilon and Richard A. Epstein

Roger Pilon is vice president for legal affairs at the Cato Institute and director of Cato's Center for Constitutional Studies. Richard A. Epstein is a law professor at New York University Law School and a senior fellow at the Hoover Institution, as well as a senior lecturer at the University of Chicago.

President Barack Obama is under harsh attack for stating the obvious: No amount of government ingenuity will guarantee the American people 100 percent security, 100 percent privacy and zero inconvenience. He was answering a burst of more heated responses from left and right alike to the "news" that for years the National Security Agency [NSA] has been collecting metadata about Americans' phone calls and certain foreign Internet communications.

A Constitutional Balance

Legally, the president is on secure footing under the Patriot Act, which Congress passed shortly after 9/11 and has since reauthorized by large bipartisan majorities. As he stressed, the program has enjoyed the continued support of all three branches of the federal government. It has been free of political abuse since its inception. And as he rightly added, this nation has real problems if its people, at least here, can't trust the combined actions of the executive branch and the Congress, backstopped by federal judges sworn to protect our individual liberties secured by the Bill of Rights.

Roger Pilon and Richard A. Epstein, "NSA Surveillance in Perspective," *Chicago Tribune*, June 12, 2013. Copyright © 2013 PARS INTERNATIONAL. All Rights Reserved. Reproduced by permission.

In asking for our trust, Obama would be on stronger ground, of course, if the NSA controversy had not followed hard on the heels of the ongoing Benghazi, IRS and AP/Fox News scandals—to say nothing of Attorney General Eric Holder's problems. But give Obama due credit: We can recall no other instance in which he announced publicly that the responsibilities of his office have changed his mind. And for the better—here's why.

The government does not know—as some have charged—whether you've called your psychiatrist, lawyer or lover.

In domestic and foreign affairs, the basic function of government is to protect our liberty, without unnecessarily violating that liberty in the process. The text of the Fourth Amendment grasps that essential trade-off by allowing searches, but not "unreasonable" ones. That instructive, albeit vague, accommodation has led courts to craft legal rules that, first, define what a search is and, second, indicate the circumstances under which one is justified. In the realm of foreign intelligence gathering, recognizing the need for secrecy and their own limitations, judges have shown an acute awareness of the strength of the public interest in national security. They have rightly deferred to Congress and the executive branch, allowing executive agencies to engage in the limited surveillance that lies at the opposite pole from ransacking a single person's sensitive papers for political purposes.

That deference is especially appropriate now that Congress, through the Patriot Act, has set a delicate balance that enables the executive branch to carry out its basic duty to protect us from another 9/11 while respecting our privacy as much as possible. Obviously, reasonable people can have reasonable differences over how that balance is struck. But on this question, political deliberation has done its job, because everyone on both sides of the aisle is seeking the right constitutional balance.

No Instance of Government Abuse

In 1979, in *Smith v. Maryland*, the U.S. Supreme Court addressed that balance when it held that using a pen register to track telephone numbers did not count as an invasion of privacy, even in ordinary criminal cases. That's just what the government is doing here on a grand scale. The metadata it examines in its effort to uncover suspicious patterns enables it to learn the numbers called, the locations of the parties, and the lengths of the calls. The government does not know—as some have charged—whether you've called your psychiatrist, lawyer or lover. The names linked to the phone numbers are not available to the government before a court grants a warrant on proof of probable cause, just as the Fourth Amendment requires. Indeed, once that warrant is granted to examine content, the content can be used only for national security issues, not even ordinary police work.

As the president said, the process involves some necessary loss of privacy. But it's trivial, certainly in comparison to the losses that would have arisen if the government had failed to discern the pattern that let it thwart the 2009 New York subway bombing plot by Colorado airport shuttle driver Najibullah Zazi, an Afghan-American, who was prosecuted and ultimately pleaded guilty.

The critics miss the forest for the trees. Yes, government officials might conceivably misuse some of the trillions of bits of metadata they examine using sophisticated algorithms. But one abuse is no pattern of abuses. And even one abuse is not likely to happen given the safeguards in place. The cumulative weight of the evidence attests to the soundness of the program. The critics would be more credible if they could identify a pattern of government abuses. But after 12 years of continuous practice, they can't cite even a single case. We should be thankful that here, at least, government has done its job and done it well.

Limited Surveillance of Americans' Communications Is Constitutional

Privacy and Civil Liberties Oversight Board

The Privacy and Civil Liberties Oversight Board is an independent agency within the executive branch established by the Implementing Recommendations of the 9/11 Commission Act of 2007.

Evaluating the constitutionality of the Section 702 [of the Foreign Intelligence Surveillance Act (FISA)] program poses unique challenges. Unlike the typical Fourth Amendment inquiry, where the legitimacy of "a particular search or seizure" is judged "in light of the particular circumstances" of that case, evaluating the government's implementation of Section 702 requires assessing a complex surveillance *program*—one that entails many separate decisions to monitor large numbers of individuals, resulting in the annual collection of hundreds of millions of communications of different types, obtained through a variety of methods, pursuant to multiple foreign intelligence imperatives, and involving four intelligence agencies that each have their own rules governing how they may handle and use the communications that are acquired.

The Fourth Amendment

Further complicating the analysis, the constitutional interests at stake are not those of the persons targeted for surveillance under Section 702, all of whom lack Fourth Amendment rights because they are foreigners located outside of the United States.

Privacy and Civil Liberties Oversight Board, "Report on the Surveillance Program Operated Pursuant to Section 702 of the Foreign Intelligence Surveillance Act," July 2, 2014, pp. 86–97. © Privacy and Civil Liberties Oversight Board. All Rights Reserved. Reproduced by permission.

Instead, the relevant Fourth Amendment interests are those of the U.S. persons whose communications may be acquired despite not themselves having been targeted for surveillance.

It has long been the rule that wiretapping conducted within the United States for criminal or other domestic purposes is presumptively unreasonable under the Fourth Amendment unless the government has obtained a warrant based on probable cause.

Although U.S. persons and other persons in the United States may not be targeted under Section 702, operation of the program nevertheless results in the government acquiring some telephone and Internet communications involving U.S. persons, potentially in large numbers. . . . [This] acquisition can occur in four main situations:

1. A U.S. person communicates by telephone or Internet with a foreigner located abroad who has been targeted. The government refers to this as "incidental" collection.

2. A U.S. person sends or receives an Internet communication that is routed internationally and that includes a reference to a selector such as an email address used by a foreigner who has been targeted. The government refers to this as "about" collection.

3. A U.S. person sends or receives an Internet communication that is embedded within the same "transaction" as a different communication that meets the requirements for acquisition (because it is to or from a targeted foreigner or includes a reference to the communications identifier of a targeted foreigner). The government refers to these transactions containing more than one separate communication as "multiple-communication transactions" or "MCTs."

4. A U.S. person's communications are acquired by mistake due to a targeting error, an implementation error, or a technological malfunction. The government refers to this as "inadvertent" collection.

Any Fourth Amendment assessment of the Section 702 program must take into account the cumulative privacy intrusions and risks of all four categories above, together with the limits and protections built into the program that mitigate them. . . .

Privacy in Telephone and Internet Communications

The Fourth Amendment protects the right of the people "to be secure in their persons, houses, papers, and effects." It thus prohibits "unreasonable searches and seizures" by the government, and it specifies that a warrant authorizing a search or seizure may issue only "upon probable cause, supported by Oath or affirmation, and particularly describing the place to be searched, and the persons or things to be seized." A search occurs not only where the government intrudes on a person's tangible private property to obtain information, but also where "the government violates a subjective expectation of privacy that society recognizes as reasonable."

Because individuals who are protected by the Constitution have a reasonable expectation of privacy in their telephone conversations, it has long been the rule that wiretapping conducted within the United States for criminal or other domestic purposes is presumptively unreasonable under the Fourth Amendment unless the government has obtained a warrant based on probable cause. While the Supreme Court has not expressly ruled on the extent of Fourth Amendment protection for Internet communications, lower courts have concluded that emails are functionally analogous to mailed letters and that therefore their contents cannot be examined by the government without a warrant. The same may be true for other, similarly private forms of Internet communication, although this question awaits further development by the courts.

[FISA] established a framework for foreign intelligence surveillance under which the executive branch obtains warrant-like orders from the FISA court before engaging in surveillance that falls within the ambit of the statute.

Under the authority of Section 702, the government collects telephone and Internet communications without obtaining individual judicial warrants for the specific people it targets. Decisions about which telephone and Internet communications to collect are made by executive branch personnel without court review. While the FISC [FISA court] plays a role in overseeing the categories of foreign intelligence the government seeks, the procedures it employs, and its adherence to statutory and constitutional limits, the court has no part in approving individual targeting decisions.

"Although as a general matter, warrantless searches are *per se* unreasonable under the Fourth Amendment, there are a few specifically established and well-delineated exceptions to that general rule." And while wiretapping and other forms of domestic electronic surveillance generally require a warrant, the Supreme Court has left open the question of whether "safeguards other than prior authorization by a magistrate would satisfy the Fourth Amendment in a situation involving the national security" and "the activities of foreign powers."

A Foreign Intelligence Exception

In other words, there may be a "foreign intelligence exception" to the warrant requirement permitting the executive branch to conduct wiretapping and other forms of electronic surveillance without judicial approval. The Supreme Court has not decided whether such an exception exists, in part because the 1978 enactment of the Foreign Intelligence Surveillance Act

("FISA") forestalled the question: the Act established a framework for foreign intelligence surveillance under which the executive branch obtains warrant-like orders from the FISA court before engaging in surveillance that falls within the ambit of the statute.

While the Supreme Court has not spoken, lower courts evaluating surveillance conducted before the enactment of FISA addressed the existence of a foreign intelligence exception, and every court to decide the question recognized such an exception. More recently the Foreign Intelligence Surveillance Court of Review concluded that a foreign intelligence exception permitted warrantless surveillance "directed at a foreign power or an agent of a foreign power"—which could include U.S. citizens—under the Protect America Act, a predecessor to Section 702.

This precedent does not neatly resolve all questions about the existence and scope of a foreign intelligence exception to the warrant requirement. The Board takes no position here on the existence or scope of that exception. We note that the program's intrusion on U.S. persons' privacy is reduced by its focus on targeting individually selected foreigners located outside the United States from whom the government reasonably expects to obtain foreign intelligence—and by the government's employment of oversight mechanisms to help ensure adherence to those limitations. Unlike the warrantless surveillance of the pre-FISA era, U.S. persons and others in the United States cannot be targeted under this program, and therefore the government never will be permitted to collect and retain their entire communications history. Instead, the government will have access only to those scattered communications that occur between a U.S. person and a targeted overseas foreigner, or that are acquired through "about" collection or as part of an MCT (which are subject to special limitations on retention and use). Moreover, the fact that the people targeted under Section 702 are situated in foreign countries may often make it difficult and time-consuming for the government to assemble documentation about them sufficient to obtain independent judicial approval for surveillance—while those targets' lack of Fourth Amendment rights militates against any legal obligation to obtain such approval or to strictly limit targeting to foreign powers and their agents.

The framework of Section 702 . . . includes a role for the judiciary in ensuring compliance with statutory and constitutional limits, albeit a more circumscribed role than the approval of individual surveillance requests.

The "Reasonableness" Framework

"Even if a warrant is not required, a search is not beyond Fourth Amendment scrutiny; for it must be reasonable in its scope and manner of execution." Thus, "even though the foreign intelligence exception applies in a given case, governmental action intruding on individual privacy interests must comport with the Fourth Amendment's reasonableness requirement." The absence of a warrant requirement simply means that, "rather than employing a *per se* rule of unreasonableness," privacy concerns and governmental interests must be balanced to determine if the intrusion is reasonable.

"Whether a search is reasonable," therefore, "is determined by assessing, on the one hand, the degree to which it intrudes upon an individual's privacy and, on the other, the degree to which it is needed for the promotion of legitimate governmental interests." Making this determination requires considering the "totality of the circumstances."

Applying this test to a program of intelligence gathering demands "sensitivity both to the government's right to protect itself from unlawful subversion and attack and to the citizen's right to be secure in his privacy against unreasonable government intrusion." When considering surveillance directed at national security threats, particularly those of a foreign nature, it is appropriate to "begin the inquiry by noting that the President of the United States has the fundamental duty, under Art. II, s 1, of the Constitution, to 'preserve, protect and defend the Constitution of the United States,'" and that "[i]mplicit in that duty is the power to protect our government against those who would subvert or overthrow it by unlawful means." More broadly, the government's interest in protecting national security "is of the highest order of magnitude."

The government has acknowledged that the Fourth Amendment rights of U.S. persons are affected when their communications are acquired under Section 702 incidentally or otherwise.

The Balancing of Privacy and Security

Additional consideration is due to the fact that the executive branch, acting under Section 702, is not exercising its Article II power unilaterally, but rather is implementing a statutory scheme enacted by Congress after public deliberation regarding the proper balance between the imperatives of privacy and national security. By establishing a statutory framework for surveillance conducted within the United States but exclusively targeting overseas foreigners, subject to certain limits and oversight mechanisms, "Congress sought to accommodate and advance both the government's interest in pursuing legitimate intelligence activity and the individual's interest in freedom from improper government intrusion." The framework of Section 702, moreover, includes a role for the judiciary in ensuring compliance with statutory and constitutional limits, albeit a more circumscribed role than the approval of individual surveillance requests. Where, as here, "the powers of all three branches of government—in short, the whole of federal authority"—are involved in establishing and monitoring the parameters of an intelligence-gathering activity, the Fourth Amendment calls for a different calculus than when the executive branch acts alone.

Furthermore, the hostile activities of terrorist organizations and other foreign entities are prone to being geographically dispersed, long-term in their planning, conducted in foreign languages or in code, and coordinated in large part from locations outside the reach of the United States. Accordingly, "complex, wide-ranging, and decentralized organizations, such as al Qaeda, warrant sustained and intense monitoring in order to understand their features and identify their members."

On the other side of the coin, the acquisition of private communications intrudes on Fourth Amendment interests. Even though U.S. persons and persons located in the United States are subject to having their telephone conversations collected only when they communicate with a targeted foreigner located abroad, the program nevertheless gains access to numerous personal conversations of U.S. persons that were carried on under an expectation of privacy. Email communications to and from U.S. persons, which the FISA court has said are akin to "papers" protected under the Fourth Amendment, are also subject to collection in a variety of circumstances. Digital tools enable the government to query the repository of collected communications to locate communications involving a given person in search of foreign intelligence or evidence of a crime. . . .

A Holistic Assessment

The government has acknowledged that the Fourth Amendment rights of U.S. persons are affected when their communications are acquired under Section 702 incidentally or otherwise, and it has echoed the FISA court's observation that the implementation of adequate minimization procedures is part of what makes the collection reasonable.

An important ramification of this holistic approach is that concerns about post-collection practices such as the use of queries to search for the communications of specific U.S. persons cannot be dismissed on the basis that the communications were "lawfully collected." Rather, whether Section 702 collection is constitutionally reasonable in the first place, and hence "lawful," depends on the reasonableness of the surveillance regime as a whole, including whether its rules affecting the acquisition, use, dissemination, and retention of the communications of U.S. persons appropriately balance the government's valid interests with the privacy of U.S. persons. . . .

In the Board's view, the core of this program—acquiring the communications of specifically targeted foreign persons who are located outside the United States, upon a belief that those persons are likely to communicate foreign intelligence, using specific communications identifiers, subject to FISA court-approved targeting rules that have proven to be accurate in targeting persons outside the United States, and subject to multiple layers of rigorous oversight—fits within the totality of the circumstances test for reasonableness as it has been defined by the courts to date.

Outside of this fundamental core, certain aspects of the Section 702 program raise questions about whether its impact on U.S. persons pushes the program over the edge into constitutional unreasonableness. Such aspects include the scope of the incidental collection of U.S. persons' communications, the use of "about" collection to acquire Internet communications that are neither to nor from the target of surveillance, the collection of MCTs that predictably will include U.S. persons' Internet communications unrelated to the purpose of the surveillance, the use of database queries to search the information collected under the program for the communications of specific U.S. persons, and the possible use of communications acquired under the program for criminal assessments, investigations, or proceedings that have no relationship to foreign intelligence.

These features of the Section 702 program, and their cumulative potential effects on the privacy of U.S. persons, push the entire program close to the line of constitutional reasonableness. At the very least, too much expansion in the collection of U.S. persons' communications or the uses to which those communications are put may push the program over the line. The response if any feature tips the program over the line is not to discard the entire program; instead, it is to address that specific feature.

Domestic Surveillance Violates Constitutional Principles

Jonathan Schell

Jonathan Schell was an author known for his work campaigning against nuclear weapons. He died in March of 2014.

A school of fish swims peacefully in the ocean. Out of sight, a net is spread beneath it. At the edges of the net is a circle of fishing boats. Suddenly, the fishermen yank up the edges of the net, and in an instant the calm, open ocean becomes a boiling caldron, an exitless, rapidly shrinking prison in which the fish thrash in vain for freedom and life.

The Growth in Surveillance

Increasingly, the American people are like this school of fish in the moments before the net is pulled up. The net in question is of course the Internet and associated instruments of data collection, and the fishermen are corporations and the government. That is, to use the more common metaphor, we have come to live alongside the machinery of a turnkey tyranny. As we now know, thanks to the courageous whistle-blower Edward Snowden, the National Security Agency [NSA] has been secretly ordering Verizon to sweep up and hand over all the metadata from the phone calls of millions of its customers: phone numbers, duration of calls, routing information and sometimes the location of the callers. Thanks to Snowden, we also know that unknown volumes of like information are being extracted from Internet and computer companies, including Microsoft, Yahoo, Google, Facebook, PalTalk, AOL, Skype, YouTube and Apple.

The first thing to note about these data is that a mere generation ago, they did not exist. They are a new power in our midst, flowing from new technology, waiting to be picked up; and power, as always, creates temptation, especially for the already powerful. Our cellphones track our whereabouts. Our communications pass through centralized servers and are saved and kept for a potential eternity in storage banks, from which they can be recovered and examined. Our purchases and contacts and illnesses and entertainments are tracked and agglomerated. If we are arrested, even our DNA can be taken and stored by the state. Today, alongside each one of us, there exists a second, electronic self, created in part by us, in part by others. This other self has become de facto public property, owned chiefly by immense data-crunching corporations, which use it for commercial purposes. Now government is reaching its hand into those corporations for its own purposes, creating a brand-new domain of the state-corporate complex.

It's not that the legislative and judicial branches are not involved; it's that each, in its own way, has abandoned its appointed constitutional role.

Surveillance of people on this scale turns basic liberties—above all the Fourth Amendment, which protects citizens against unreasonable search and seizure—into a dead letter. Government officials, it is true, assure us that they will never pull the edges of the net tight. They tell us that although they *could* know everything about us, they won't decide to. They'll let the information sit unexamined in the electronic vaults. But history, whether of our country or others, teaches that only a fool would place faith in such assurances. What one president refrains from doing the next will do; what is left undone in peacetime is done when a crisis comes.

The System of Checks and Balances

The executive branch offers a similar assurance about its claimed right to kill American and foreign citizens at its sole discretion. But to accept such assurances as the guarantee of basic liberties would be to throw away bedrock principles of our constitutional order. If there is any single political idea that deserves to be called quintessentially American, it is the principle that government power must be balanced and checked by other government power, which is why federal power is balanced by state power and is itself divided into three branches.

The officials—most notably President [Barack] Obama—have assured us that this system is intact, that the surveillance programs are "under very strict supervision by all three branches of government," in Obama's words. But the briefest examination of the record rebuts the claim. In this matter, the interactions of the three branches are a cause not for reassurance but for deeper alarm. It's not that the legislative and judicial branches are not involved; it's that each, in its own way, has abandoned its appointed constitutional role.

The three branches, far from checking one another's power or protecting the rights of Americans, entered one after another into collusion to violate them.

The story arguably begins with George W. Bush's end run around the legal system after the terrorist attacks of 2001, when, in complete disregard of the law, he initiated warrantless domestic surveillance by the NSA. So clearly illegal and extreme was this program that high-ranking officials of his administration, including James Comey, deputy attorney general, and Robert Mueller, director of the FBI [Federal Bureau of Investigation], threatened to resign. Bush backed off some of the measures, and the confrontation did not become known until much later.

What happened then? Did Congress check this executive usurpation? Did it castigate Bush, forbid the crimes, hold his officials accountable? It did not. It adopted the worst features of the Bush program as law, in the Protect America Act of 2007 and the Foreign Intelligence Surveillance Amendments Act of 2008 [FISA]; it also immunized from legal repercussions corporations that had secretly knuckled under to Bush's wrongdoing. Far from correcting the abuses, Congress institutionalized them. At the same time, it supported the executive branch's cloak of secrecy over those abuses and the classification of the legal opinions of the FISA court, whose rulings have given legal protection to the new surveillance programs. The Obama administration's legal opinions on the practices are also classified.

As for the judicial branch, it happens that in 1979, the Supreme Court ruled that the sort of metadata collected from Verizon is not covered by the Fourth Amendment. (In fairness, there is no sign that the Court anticipated or meant to approve the sort of indiscriminate dragnet of metadata now under way. Thus, a lawsuit recently brought by the ACLU [American Civil Liberties Union] to stop this has a chance of succeeding.) The FISA court almost never refuses government requests. James Bamford, an expert on NSA surveillance, has characterized this institution as "a super hush-hush surveillance court that is virtually impotent."

Our system of checks and balances has gone into reverse. The three branches, far from checking one another's power or protecting the rights of Americans, entered one after another into collusion to violate them, even to the extent of immunizing the wrongdoers. Balanced, checked power has become fused power—exactly what the founders of this country feared above all else. The political parties have been no more useful as checks than the branches of government; their leaderships stand together protecting the abuses, though individual senators, including Jeff Merkley and Ron Wyden, have proposed sensible reforms.

The Need for Counterrevolution

Finally, even elections have proven ineffective: the voters chose a president who taught constitutional law running on a platform of stopping civil liberties abuses; but he has become the author of new abuses. Even now, his soothing demeanor and reputation for liberalism ("Change we can believe in") confuses and thwarts those who otherwise would be reacting with anger.

What should Americans do when all official channels are unresponsive or dysfunctional? Are we, as people used to say, in a revolutionary situation? Shall we man the barricades? The situation is a little more peculiar than that. There is a revolution afoot, but it is not one in the streets; it is one that is being carried out by the government against the fundamental law of the land. That this insurrection against the constitutional order by officials sworn to uphold it includes legal opinions and legislation only makes it the more radical and dangerous. In other words, the government is in stealthy insurrection against the letter and the spirit of the law.

What's needed is counterrevolution—an American restoration, returning to and reaffirming the principles on which the Republic was founded. Edward Snowden, for one, knew what to do. He saw that when government as a whole goes rogue, the only force with a chance of bringing it back into line is the public. He has helped make this possible by letting the public know the abuses that are being carried out in its name. Civil disobedients are of two kinds: those inspired by universal principles, and those inspired by national traditions. Each has its strengths. Julian Assange of WikiLeaks is the first kind; Snowden, the second. Asked why he had done what he did, Snowden replied, "I am neither traitor nor hero. I am an American." He based his actions on the finest traditions of this country, which its current leaders have abandoned but which, he hopes, the current generation of Americans still share. In the weeks and months ahead, we'll find out whether he was right.

The NSA's Metadata Surveillance Program Is Unconstitutional

Geoffrey R. Stone

Geoffrey R. Stone is the Edward H. Levi Distinguished Service Professor at the University of Chicago.

Under section 215 of the Foreign Intelligence Surveillance Act, as interpreted by the Foreign Intelligence Surveillance Court, the NSA [National Security Agency] is authorized to obtain from telephone service providers on a daily basis the calling records of millions of Americans. The calling records, or metadata, consist of the phone numbers called by a particular phone number and the phone numbers that have called that particular number. They do not include any information about the identities of the individuals or the contents of the calls. The NSA holds this metadata in a very large database for a period of five years, after which it is expunged.

The Government's Database

Whenever NSA analysts have reasonable and articulable suspicion that a particular phone number is associated with a person involved in terrorist activity, they can "query" the database to determine what phone numbers the suspect phone number has been in touch with. This is the *only* purpose for which the NSA may access the database.

In 2012, the NSA queried a total of 288 phone numbers. Based on these queries, the NSA found 16 instances in which a suspect phone number was directly or indirectly in touch with another phone number that the NSA independently suspected of being associated with terrorist activity. In such cases, the NSA turns the information over to the FBI [Federal Bureau of Investigation] for further investigation.

The question . . . is whether this "search" process is "unreasonable" within the meaning of the Fourth Amendment.

In terms of the "connect the dots" metaphor, the purpose of the program is not so much to discover new "dots" but to determine if there are connections between two or more already suspect "dots." For example, if a phone number belonging to a terrorist suspect in Pakistan is found to have called a phone number in the United States that the government independently suspects belongs to a person involved in possible terrorist activity, alarm bells (figuratively) go off very loudly, alerting the government to the need for immediate attention.

It is important to note that the program does not allow the NSA or anyone else in the government to access the metadata for *any* purpose other than what I have just described. There are rigorous safeguards in place both internally through the NSA's Office of General Counsel and externally pursuant to oversight by the Department of Justice, the congressional intelligence committees, and the Foreign Intelligence Surveillance Court to ensure that no one accesses the database for any other purpose.

The question, then, is whether this "search" process is "unreasonable" within the meaning of the Fourth Amendment.

The Fourth Amendment

As a general rule, the Supreme Court has held that conventional "searches"—for example, when the police rummage through a person's home, wiretap his phone calls, or read his mail—are presumptively "unreasonable" and therefore unconstitutional unless the government first obtains a judicial warrant based on a finding that there is probable cause to believe that the search will turn up evidence of a crime.

The NSA's bulk telephony metadata program clearly cannot pass muster under that standard. It requires neither a warrant nor a finding of probable cause when it collects the call records of millions of individuals, and it requires neither a warrant nor a finding of probable cause when NSA analysts query the database to investigate the call records of specific individuals whom they suspect of terrorist activity.

Certainly, the government's interest in protecting the national security is more important than its interest in, say, preventing drunk driving and housing code violations.

That does not end the matter, however, because the Supreme Court has held that *many* forms of searches are "reasonable" even if they do not satisfy the warrant and/or probable cause requirements. For example, the court has held that the government can inspect *all* homes in a town for possible housing code violations—without any showing of probable cause to believe that any *specific* home has such a violation. It has held that the government can require *all* persons boarding an airplane to pass through a magnetometer—without any showing of probable cause to believe that any *specific* person is carrying a weapon. It has held that the police can use roadblocks in which they stop *every* car approaching a particular checkpoint in order to check for drunken drivers—without any showing of probable cause to believe that any *specific* person is drunk. It has held that a police officer can frisk an individual he has stopped for questioning if the officer has reasonable and articulable grounds to suspect that the person is armed and presently dangerous—without any showing of probable cause to believe that the individual has either committed a crime or possesses a weapon.

103

The question, then, is whether the bulk telephony metadata program is another example of a search that is "reasonable" even though it requires neither probable cause nor a warrant. In addressing this question, it is helpful to keep in mind that the metadata program, unlike most searches, has two distinct elements—(a) the collection and storage of the metadata, and (b) the querying of the database. This complicates the analysis.

With respect to the first part of the program—the collection and storage of the telephony metadata, it is worth noting at the outset that the government routinely collects all sorts of data about us. It collects information about such matters as taxes, employment, health, travel, families, census data, etc. One might argue that, if those types of data collection are not unconstitutional, then the same should be true of the government's collection of telephony metadata under section 215. An important difference, however, is that unlike most other data-collection activities, the section 215 program gathers the metadata precisely for the purpose of sniffing out possible wrongdoing. In that sense, it more directly implicates the concerns underlying the Fourth Amendment than most other information-gathering programs.

The Reasonableness of Surveillance

In my judgment, and the law here is quite unsettled, the reasonableness of any particular program of government information collection should turn on four primary factors: (1) How important is it to collect the information? (2) How private is the information collected? (3) How will the information be used? (4) How confident are we that the information will be used only for proper purposes?

How do these factors play out in the collection and storage of telephony metadata under section 215?

(1) The metadata is collected under this program for a clearly legitimate and, indeed, important purpose. Protecting

the national security is surely a compelling government interest, and the President's Review Group found that the metadata program is useful, if not essential, to achieving this goal. Certainly, the government's interest in protecting the national security is more important than its interest in, say, preventing drunk driving and housing code violations.

(2) Defenders of the program maintain that it does not threaten significant privacy interests because it deals only with metadata and not with the contents of the phone calls. The collection of metadata, they argue, is analogous to the use of magnetometers at airports (as compared, say, to a requirement that all passengers must be strip-searched, which presumably would be deemed "unreasonable"). Metadata may in fact reveal less private information than the contents of the calls, but as I have explained in prior posts, and as the President's Review Group clearly found, comprehensive inquiries into an individual's telephone calling records can reveal a huge amount of highly personal information about an a individual's private life.

(3) For that reason, if the government were authorized to use the database to investigate the personal lives of ordinary Americans, the telephony metadata program would clearly be "unreasonable." But under the section 215 program, the government is authorized to access the metadata for only a very specific, very narrow, and carefully targeted purpose. It cannot legally access the metadata for any purpose other than to "connect the dots" between one suspected terrorist and another. It cannot legally access the database to learn *anything* about the private lives of ordinary Americans. It can legally use the database only to determine if suspected terrorist X is in contact with suspected terrorist Y. Period. Any other use of the data is forbidden. This is an essential feature of the program, and it sharply limits its potential threat to individual privacy.

(4) Despite such limitations, however, there is always the danger of abuse. When the government has access to such information, there is always a risk that it will exploit the information for a broad range of impermissible purposes. There is always the possibility that some future J. Edgar Hoover or Richard Nixon will turn this extraordinary pool of private information to ignoble ends. Moreover, even in the absence of actual abuse, individuals may fear that the government will use this information—illegally—to their detriment, and this in itself can affect their behavior in ways that seriously infringe on individual freedom. The safeguards in place to prevent such abuse are therefore critical to the "reasonableness" of the program. In the current system, the safeguards that now exist to prevent such abuse are quite extensive. But no system of safeguards is perfect, and in the wrong hands serious harm is always possible.

As in other searches, the decision to search [the telephony database] should be made by a neutral and detached judge rather than by a government official engaged in the adversarial process of ferreting out the "bad guys."

The Importance of Judicial Determination

On this particular issue—which in my view is central to the "reasonableness" of the program, the President's Review Group—which addressed this question from the standpoint of public policy rather than constitutionality—recommended that at least two additional safeguards are necessary. First, the metadata should be held for a period of only two rather than five years, thereby limiting the potential harm to privacy. Second, the metadata should be held, not by the government, but by a private entity—either by the phone companies themselves or by a newly-created private agency. These additional safeguards are necessary to reduce both the risk of abuse and the fear of abuse. But with these additional safeguards in place, the collection of metadata, used solely for the purpose currently authorized, seems to me to meet the test of "reasonableness."

The second component of the section 215 program focuses on the circumstances in which the government can query the database. At present, the NSA is authorized to query the database if NSA analysts find that there are reasonable and articulable grounds to believe that a particular phone number is associated with terrorist activity.

There are two possible objections to this procedure. First, one might argue that, to meet with requirements of the Fourth Amendment, the NSA should not be able to query the database unless a *judge*—rather than an NSA analyst—makes the critical determination that there are reasonable and articulable grounds to believe that a particular phone number is connected to terrorist activity. There is no good reason to dispense with the requirement of a judicial determination, at least in the absence of an emergency. As in other searches, the decision to search should be made by a neutral and detached judge rather than by a government official engaged in the adversarial process of ferreting out the "bad guys." The absence of such a requirement, in my judgment, violates the Fourth Amendment.

Second, although reasonable people can certainly differ on this, I am inclined to think that the "reasonable and articulable suspicion" standard meets the test of "reasonableness" in this context because of the very narrow and targeted nature of the inquiry—that is, the *only* information that can lawfully be disclosed as a result of a query is that a suspected terrorist has been in touch, directly or indirectly, with another suspected terrorist.

In conclusion, then, in my judgment the existing program is unconstitutional. As currently structured, it violates the Fourth Amendment's requirement of "reasonableness." On the other hand, it should be possible for the government to correct the deficiencies in the program in a manner that both preserves its legitimate value and substantially mitigates the risks to privacy that it currently poses.

There are those who maintain that this program is obviously constitutional and those who maintain that it is obviously unconstitutional. They are both wrong. There is nothing "obvious" about this. If this ever gets to the Supreme Court, it will be interesting.

NSA Surveillance Program Is Unreasonable, Unwarranted, and Unconstitutional

Daniel Bier

Daniel Bier is the publisher and executive editor of The Skeptical Libertarian.

In his latest post at Ricochet.com, libertarian law professor Richard Epstein responded to criticism of his earlier op-ed, co-authored with Cato's Roger Pilon, defending the NSA's [National Security Agency's] secret data-gathering programs. While conceding factual errors on a couple of points, Epstein maintained his core argument that the mass surveillance of millions of Americans' internet and telecommunications data constitutes both a necessary and reasonable search, because of the continuing threat of terrorism.

The Threat of Terrorism

"The amorphous nature of the threat requires extensive surveillance until we can identify responsible parties against whom direct action can be taken. . . . It makes no sense to limit metadata searches to known suspects when unknown suspects may well pose the central danger," Epstein writes. "Therefore, the correct approach is to cast the net wide by tracing connections, invoking more intrusive searches only when justified by concrete evidence. . . . But curtailing or eliminating general surveillance for abstract concerns about abuse is a dangerous, if not reckless, approach."

This is certainly an extraordinary claim. Regardless of the crime, "unknown suspects" may *always* pose a greater danger than known ones, by mere virtue of their anonymity. The fact police haven't identified a suspect yet does not make everyone a suspect, nor does a 0.00001% chance of any given individual being a terrorist make it "reasonable" to suspend normal civil liberties protections for the entire population.

"National security issues," even in the aggregate, pose a much smaller risk to the lives of Americans than domestic crimes committed every day by US citizens against their neighbors.

In fact, the less probable the threat, the more "amorphous" it becomes, and the harder it is to find the responsible parties. By this logic, the *least* likely threats justify the *most* serious infringements on the *largest* number of people. Since 1968, over 800,000 people have been murdered in the United States; including 9/11, only 3,245 have been killed in terrorist incidents. The threat of terrorism is orders of magnitude smaller than the threat of murder, but we are to believe that, not *in spite* of that fact, but *because* of it, we must endure breaches of privacy to catch terrorists that we would never allow to catch murderers.

A Future-Crime Program

Indeed, in his original op-ed, Epstein defended the NSA program on the grounds that the data collected *couldn't* be used for ordinary law enforcement purposes, like catching murderers, rapists, or tax-evaders: "The content can be used only for national security issues, not even ordinary police work."

He was just wrong about that—information gathered under the Foreign Intelligence Surveillance Act [FISA] can be used for non-national security related crimes—but even if it couldn't, on what basis could you justify this inversion of priorities? "National security issues," even in the aggregate, pose a much smaller risk to the lives of Americans than domestic crimes committed every day by US citizens against their neighbors.

Furthermore, notice who these surveillance programs are trying to identify: "unknown suspects." The NSA isn't, mainly, trying to find the guilty parties behind specific crimes: it is trying to locate terrorists *before* they commit terrorism, by linking their communications to known bad actors or by storing tons of data that can *later* be accessed for data-mining when the government desires to look up associations of a particular individual. The reason why these individuals are, by definition, unknown is that we are looking for suspects of crimes that haven't been committed yet. It is a future-crime program.

A Poor Justification

The fact there *may* be someone, somewhere, *thinking* about doing bad things does not give the government probable cause to collect, store, and analyze all of our telecommunications records. Yet, this appeared to be the logic of the secret FISA court, which, in 2006, radically expanded the "business records" provision of the Patriot Act, which allows the FBI [Federal Bureau of Investigation] to compel companies to turn over specific customer data relevant to a terrorism investigation, to cover the entirety of a telephone company's call database. All of your private communications are now considered relevant to terrorism investigations, because it may be "helpful," at some point, to the government's interest in identifying suspects.

At the very least, the burden of proof is on the government to demonstrate it could not locate such persons using traditional, targeted investigatory tools and that the tradeoff in privacy is worth the reduced risk of terrorism. But we have had no such informed debate, and *cannot* while the government refuses to share important details about how these programs work and what allegedly indispensable role they played in stopping terror attacks. The government's response to the public's concerns has been "trust us," with the implication that it need not reciprocate.

Fear-mongering about nuclear bombs and ticking clocks aside, the eternal, omnipresent, and amorphous threat of bad things happening should not create a permanent state of "exigent circumstances" which supersede ordinary 4th Amendment protections. If the infinitesimal risk of terrorism can reasonably justify suspending our right to privacy in this way, anything can justify anything.

CHAPTER 4

How Should Government Surveillance Be Regulated?

Overview: Americans Disapprove of Government Surveillance Programs

Frank Newport

Frank Newport is editor-in-chief of Gallup and author of Polling Matters: Why Leaders Must Listen to the Wisdom of the People.

More Americans disapprove (53%) than approve (37%) of the federal government agency program that as part of its efforts to investigate terrorism obtained records from U.S. telephone and Internet companies to "compile telephone call logs and Internet communications."

These results are from a June 10-11 [2013] Gallup poll. Although the current survey context was different, these results are similar to those obtained in a May 2006 Gallup poll measuring support for a government program that "obtained records from three of the largest U.S. telephone companies in order to create a database of billions of telephone numbers dialed by Americans." In that survey, 43% approved and 51% disapproved.

There are significant partisan differences in views of the government's program to obtain call logs and Internet communication. Democrats are more likely to approve, by 49% to 40%. Independents (34% vs. 56%) and Republicans (32% to 63%) are much more likely to disapprove than approve.

In 2006, when Gallup asked the similar question about a program that came to light at that point, Republicans were significantly more likely to approve than Democrats. The differences in partisan reaction between 2006 and 2013 reflect the party of the president under whose watch the programs were carried out at those two points in time.

A separate question included in Gallup's survey found that 35% of Americans said they would be "very concerned" about violation of their own privacy rights if the government had computerized logs of their telephone calls or Internet communications.

Twenty-one percent of Americans disapprove of the government's actions, but say there could be circumstances in which it would be right for the government to carry out such a program, yielding a combined total of 58% of all Americans who either approve or could theoretically approve under certain circumstances.

A June 9–10 [2013] CBS News poll also found a majority (58%) of Americans disapproving of the government "collecting phone records of ordinary Americans." A June 6–9 [2013] survey conducted by Pew Research Center and *The Washington Post* found that 56% of Americans said a program in which the National Security Agency "has been getting secret court orders to track telephone call records of millions of Americans in an effort to investigate terrorism" was "acceptable." The combined 58% in the Gallup survey who either approve or say there might be circumstances in which such a program would be right is similar to the acceptable percentage in the Pew/*Post* wording.

Thirty-Five Percent of Americans Very Concerned About Violation of Their Privacy Rights

A separate question included in Gallup's survey found that 35% of Americans said they would be "very concerned" about violation of their own privacy rights if the government had computerized logs of their telephone calls or Internet communications. Another 22% said they would be "somewhat concerned."

Sixty-four percent of Americans are following news about this issue very or somewhat closely, which is slightly above average for all news stories tested by Gallup over the past two decades.

Mixed Sentiment About the Leaker's Action

U.S. officials are engaged in a manhunt for Edward Snowden, the former U.S. government contractor who claimed to be the source of the leak. Americans break roughly even when asked if it was right (44%) or wrong (42%) for Snowden to share that information with the press.

A plurality of Republicans said he did the right thing in leaking the news of the surveillance programs, while a plurality of Democrats said he did the wrong thing.

Americans are more positive about the media's actions in this matter, with 59% saying it was right for *The Guardian* and *The Washington Post* newspapers to publish the information once they received it.

Implications

Results from the Gallup poll indicate that Americans have somewhat flexible views about the government's surveillance program and/or that they are still forming their opinions on the issue. A majority of Americans say that they might find the type of government surveillance program that has come to light in recent days as acceptable under some circumstances, but less than half say they approve of the program as it stands.

The reactions to these types of government programs have remained constant over the past seven years, although Republicans and Democrats have essentially flipped their attitudes over that time period, reflecting the change from Republican President George W. Bush to Democratic President Barack Obama.

Americans are divided as to whether the self-confessed leaker, Edward Snowden, is a hero or a villain, while one-third of Americans fault the press for advancing the story.

Surveillance Allowed Under the FISA Amendments Act Should Continue

John G. Malcolm and Jessica Zuckerman

John G. Malcolm is director of the Edwin Meese III Center for Legal and Judicial Studies and Jessica Zuckerman is a policy analyst at The Heritage Foundation.

In September [2012], the House of Representatives passed the reauthorization of the Foreign Intelligence Surveillance Amendments Act of 2008 (FAA), which made key updates to the authorities granted to U.S. intelligence under the Foreign Intelligence Surveillance Act (FISA). Reauthorization of the bill, which expires at the end of this year, has yet to be taken up by the Senate. Following the attention brought to the FAA by the *Clapper v. Amnesty International USA* case before the Supreme Court, the measure is now left to be considered by the Senate during the lame-duck session.

The Senate should prevent the FAA from expiring during the lame-duck session to ensure that U.S. counterterrorism officials have the tools they need to keep America safe.

FISA and Title VII

Enacted in 1978, FISA created a secret national security court to review wiretap applications for national security investigations conducted in the U.S. that involve foreign powers or their agents. With FISA, Congress recognized the need to distinguish between rigorous judicial review of intelligence surveillance efforts in the U.S. (where the Fourth Amendment

John G. Malcolm and Jessica Zuckerman, "Foreign Intelligence Surveillance Amendments Act of 2008," *Issue Brief*, no. 3370, The Heritage Foundation, November 13, 2012, pp. 1–3. © The Heritage Foundation. All Rights Reserved. Reproduced by permission.

applies) and allowing the government to conduct surveillance overseas (where the Fourth Amendment does not apply) without judicial oversight.

Individual warrants are still required if the target is a U.S. citizen regardless of where he is located and even if the government believes he is acting as a foreign agent.

These distinctions were made through the definition of "electronic surveillance." However, modern technology resulted in an increasing number of calls and e-mails passing through the U.S. in which it was not immediately clear that both ends of the communications were occurring outside the U.S. The government then expended significant manpower generating FISA court applications for surveillance against persons outside the U.S., even though Congress meant to exclude these targets when it enacted FISA.

Title VII of FISA, as added by the FAA, addressed this problem by allowing the FISA court to streamline approval for surveillance of suspected foreign state and terrorist agents without requiring an individualized application for each target. This streamlined process requires the Attorney General and the Director of National Intelligence to provide an annual certification to the FISA court identifying the categories of foreign intelligence targets subject to surveillance and certifying that all FAA requirements, including targeting and minimization procedures, have been met.

The "targeting procedures" are rules to determine whether each target is located outside the U.S. and are designed to "prevent the intentional acquisition of any communication as to which the sender and all intended recipients are known at the time of the acquisition to be located in the United States." The "minimization procedures" require that surveillance be "reasonably designed ... to minimize the acquisition and retention, and prohibit the dissemination, of nonpublicly available information concerning unconsenting United States persons."

Individual warrants are still required if the target is a U.S. citizen regardless of where he is located and even if the government believes he is acting as a foreign agent. Prior to passage of the FAA, collection of such information on U.S. citizens could be authorized by the Attorney General without court approval.

Clapper v. Amnesty International USA

On October 29, the U.S. Supreme Court heard arguments in *Clapper v. Amnesty International USA*. The only issue before the Court at this time is whether anyone has the right—or "standing," as it is technically called in legal circles—to file a lawsuit challenging the constitutionality of the wiretap provisions in the FAA.

The FAA ensures that our nation's intelligence community has the essential tools it needs to gather information necessary to stop terrorists long before American citizens are put in danger.

Within hours after the 2008 law went into effect, a group of lawyers, journalists, and human rights organizations filed a lawsuit challenging the constitutionality of Section 702 of FISA, which was added by the FAA. The plaintiffs claim that the wiretapping that is being conducted by the government pursuant to the law is so pervasive that it is highly likely that some of their telephone calls, e-mails, and other communications with clients and other contacts located in foreign countries are being intercepted and that, in order to maintain the confidentiality of those communications, they have altered the way they engage in overseas contacts at considerable expense.

The government contends that the plaintiffs lack standing. It also argues that even if the challengers prevailed in their constitutional challenge to the FAA, such a "win" would neither prevent the government from monitoring their conversations if it wanted to do so—since it has other legal authorities that it could rely upon—nor prevent other governments from monitoring such communications.

FAA and the Lame Duck

While this case was pending before the Supreme Court, the House of Representatives voted to reauthorize the FAA without revision for a period of five years, as requested by the [Barack] Obama Administration. The Senate, however, failed to act.

Now, as Congress returns in its lame-duck session, the Senate will debate two options. The Senate Select Committee on Intelligence has proposed reauthorizing the FAA without modification—exactly what the House did—while the Senate Committee on the Judiciary has proposed that the FAA be reauthorized for two-and-a-half years so as to be aligned with the other sunsetting provisions of FISA.

In a letter urging Congress to reauthorize the FAA earlier this year, Director of National Intelligence (DNI) James Clapper and Attorney General Eric Holder asserted that "intelligence collection under Title VII has produced and continues to produce significant intelligence that is vital to protect the nation against international terrorism and other threats." Indeed, the FAA ensures that our nation's intelligence community has the essential tools it needs to gather information necessary to stop terrorists long before American citizens are put in danger.

An Effective Tool Against Terrosism

Already, at least 53 publicly known terrorist plots aimed against the United States have been thwarted since 9/11. While a select few have been foiled by luck or the swift action of the

American public, the vast majority have been thwarted through the concerted efforts of U.S. and international law enforcement and intelligence.

Without the provisions of the FAA, obtaining court approval for the surveillance of potential international terrorists would be a more time-consuming and onerous process than was ever intended by Congress when it passed FISA. Moreover, contrary to arguments being made by its critics and the plaintiffs in the *Clapper* case, the FAA offers multiple levels of oversight and safeguards to ensure compliance, including:

- Standards to prevent the intentional targeting of U.S. persons;

- Procedures to minimize the inadvertent acquisition and retention of the communication of U.S. citizens;

- Semi-annual assessments of compliance by the Attorney General and DNI, as well as annual assessments by each intelligence agency presented to Congress and the FISA court; and

- Periodic oversight reviews by the Department of Justice and DNI.

Indeed, these provisions offer even greater protection than exists with regard to domestic wiretaps.

Significant advances in technology have occurred since the passage of FISA in 1978. The FAA serves to bring surveillance capabilities in line with these advancements, all while protecting the rights of American citizens and preventing abuse. When Congress returns during its lame-duck session, the Senate should ensure that the FAA is not allowed to expired [it passed and became law on December 30, 2012, set to expire at the end of 2017]. Fighting 21st-century terrorism requires that U.S. intelligence possess 21st-century tools.

Surveillance Allowed Under the FISA Amendments Act Has Gone Too Far

Ron Wyden

Ron Wyden is the senior US senator from Oregon and a member of the Democratic Party.

After 9/11, when 3,000 Americans were murdered by terrorists, there was a consensus that our government needed to take decisive action. At a time of understandable panic, Congress gave the government new surveillance authorities, but attached an expiration date to these authorities so that they could be deliberated more carefully once the immediate emergency had passed. Yet in the decade since, that law has been extended several times with no public discussion about how the law has actually been interpreted. The result: the creation of an always expanding, omnipresent surveillance state that—hour by hour—chips needlessly away at the liberties and freedoms our Founders established for us, without the benefit of actually making us any safer.

The Surveillance State

So, today I'm going to deliver another warning: If we do not seize this unique moment in our constitutional history to reform our surveillance laws and practices, we will all live to regret it. I'll have more to say about the consequences of the omnipresent surveillance state, but ... ponder that most of us have a computer in our pocket that potentially can be used to track and monitor us 24/7.

Ron Wyden, Speech on NSA Domestic Surveillance at the Center for American Progress, July 23, 2013, pp. 4–13, 15–17, 29. © US Government. All Rights Reserved. Reproduced by permission.

The combination of increasingly advanced technology with a breakdown in the checks and balances that limit government action could lead us to a surveillance state that cannot be reversed.

The secret rulings of the Foreign Intelligence Surveillance Court have interpreted the Patriot Act, as well as section 702 of the FISA statute, in some surprising ways, and these rulings are kept entirely secret from the public.

At this point, a little bit of history might be helpful. I joined the Senate Intelligence Committee in January 2001, just before 9/11. Like most senators I voted for the original Patriot Act, in part, because I was reassured that it had an expiration date that would force Congress to come back and consider these authorities more carefully when the immediate crisis had passed. As time went on, from my view on the Intelligence Committee there were developments that seemed farther and farther removed from the ideals of our Founding Fathers. This started not long after 9/11, with a Pentagon program called Total Information Awareness, which was essentially an effort to develop an ultra-large-scale domestic data-mining system. Troubled by this effort, and its not exactly modest logo of an all-seeing eye on the universe, I worked with a number of senators to shut it down. Unfortunately, this was hardly the last domestic surveillance overreach. In fact, the NSA's infamous warrantless wiretapping program was already up and running at that point, though I, and most members of the Intelligence Committee didn't learn about it until a few years later. This was part of a pattern of withholding information from Congress that persisted throughout the [George W.] Bush administration—I joined the Intelligence Committee in 2001, but I learned about the warrantless wiretapping program when you read about it in the *New York Times* in late 2005.

The Bush administration spent most of 2006 attempting to defend the warrantless wiretapping program. Once again, when the truth came out, it produced a surge of public pressure and the Bush administration announced that they would submit to oversight from Congress and the Foreign Intelligence Surveillance Court, also known as the FISA Court. Unfortunately, because the FISA Court's rulings are secret, most Americans had no idea that the Court was prepared to issue incredibly broad rulings, permitting the massive surveillance that finally made headlines last month.

It's now a matter of public record that the bulk phone records program has been operating since at least 2007. It's not a coincidence that a handful of senators have been working since then to find ways to alert the public about what has been going on. Months and years went into trying to find ways to raise public awareness about secret surveillance authorities within the confines of classification rules.

The Use of Secret Law

I and several of my colleagues have made it our mission to end the use of secret law.

When Oregonians hear the words secret law, they have come up to me and asked, "Ron, how can the law be secret? When you guys pass laws that's a public deal. I'm going to look them up online." In response, I tell Oregonians that there are effectively two Patriot Acts—the first is the one that they can read on their laptop in Medford or Portland, analyze and understand. Then there's the real Patriot Act—the secret interpretation of the law that the government is actually relying upon. The secret rulings of the Foreign Intelligence Surveillance Court have interpreted the Patriot Act, as well as section 702 of the FISA statute, in some surprising ways, and these rulings are kept entirely secret from the public. These rulings can be astoundingly broad. The one that authorizes the bulk collection of phone records is as broad as any I have ever seen.

125

This reliance of government agencies on a secret body of law has real consequences. Most Americans don't expect to know the details about ongoing sensitive military and intelligence activities, but as voters they absolutely have a need and a right to know what their government thinks it is permitted to do, so that they can ratify or reject decisions that elected officials make on their behalf. To put it another way, Americans recognize that intelligence agencies will sometimes need to conduct secret operations, but they don't think those agencies should be relying on secret law.

Without public laws, and public court rulings interpreting those laws, it is impossible to have informed public debate.

Now, some argue that keeping the meaning of surveillance laws secret is necessary, because it makes it easier to gather intelligence on terrorist groups and other foreign powers. If you follow this logic, when Congress passed the original Foreign Intelligence Surveillance Act back in the 1970s, they could have found a way to make the whole thing secret, so that Soviet agents wouldn't know what the FBI's [Federal Bureau of Investigation's] surveillance authorities were. But that's not the way you do it in America.

The Fundamental Principle of Public Law

It is a fundamental principle of American democracy that laws should not be public only when it is convenient for government officials to make them public. They should be public all the time, open to review by adversarial courts, and subject to change by an accountable legislature guided by an informed public. If Americans are not able to learn how their government is interpreting and executing the law then we have effectively eliminated the most important bulwark of our democracy. That's why, even at the height of the Cold War, when the argument for absolute secrecy was at its zenith, Congress chose to make US surveillance laws public.

Without public laws, and public court rulings interpreting those laws, it is impossible to have informed public debate. And when the American people are in the dark, they can't make fully informed decisions about who should represent them, or protest policies that they disagree with. These are fundamentals. It's Civics 101. And secret law violates those basic principles. It has no place in America.

Now let's turn to the secret court—the Foreign Intelligence Surveillance Court, the one virtually no one had heard of two months ago and now the public asks me about at the barber.

The FISA Court

When the FISA court was created as part of the 1978 FISA law its work was pretty routine. It was assigned to review government applications for wiretaps and decide whether the government was able to show probable cause. Sounds like the garden variety function of district court judges across America. In fact, their role was so much like a district court that the judges who make up the FISA Court are all current federal district court judges.

After 9/11, Congress passed the Patriot Act and the FISA Amendments Act. This gave the government broad new surveillance powers that didn't much resemble anything in either the criminal law enforcement world or the original FISA law. The FISA Court got the job of interpreting these new, unparalleled authorities of the Patriot Act and FISA Amendments Act. They chose to issue binding secret rulings that interpreted the law and the Constitution in the startling way that has come to light in the last six weeks. They were to issue the decision that the Patriot Act could be used for dragnet, bulk surveillance of law-abiding Americans.

Outside the names of the FISA court judges, virtually everything else is secret about the court. Their rulings are secret, which makes challenging them in an appeals court almost impossible. Their proceedings are secret too, but I can tell you that they are almost always one-sided. The government lawyers walk in and lay out an argument for why the government should be allowed to do something, and the Court decides based solely on the judge's assessment of the government's arguments. That's not unusual if a court is considering a routine warrant request, but it's very unusual if a court is doing major legal or constitutional analysis. I know of absolutely no other court in this country that strays so far from the adversarial process that has been part of our system for centuries.

The bulk collection of phone records significantly impacts the privacy of million of law-abiding Americans.

It may also surprise you to know that when President [Barack] Obama came to office, his administration agreed with me that these rulings needed to be made public. In the summer of 2009 I received a written commitment from the Justice Department and the Office of the Director of National Intelligence that a process would be created to start redacting and declassifying FISA Court opinions, so that the American people could have some idea of what the government believes the law allows it to do. In the last four years exactly zero opinions have been released.

The Rights of Americans

Now that we know a bit about secret law and the court that created it, let's talk about how it has diminished the rights of every American man, woman and child.

Despite the efforts of the intelligence community leadership to downplay the privacy impact of the Patriot Act collection, the bulk collection of phone records significantly impacts the privacy of million of law-abiding Americans. If you know who someone called, when they called, where they called from, and how long they talked, you lay bare the personal lives of law-abiding Americans to the scrutiny of government bureaucrats and outside contractors. . . .

Today, government officials are openly telling the press that they have the authority to effectively turn Americans' smart phones and cell phones into location-enabled homing beacons. Compounding the problem is the fact that the case law is unsettled on cell phone tracking and the leaders of the intelligence community have consistently been unwilling to state what the rights of law-abiding people are on this issue. Without adequate protections built into the law there's no way that Americans can ever be sure that the government isn't going to interpret its authorities more and more broadly, year after year, until the idea of a telescreen monitoring your every move turns from dystopia to reality.

The growth of digital technology, dramatic changes in the nature of warfare and the definition of a battlefield, and novel courts that run counter to everything the Founding Fathers imagined, make for a combustible mix.

Some would say that could never happen because there is secret oversight and secret courts that guard against it. But the fact of the matter is that senior policymakers and federal judges have deferred again and again to the intelligence agencies to decide what surveillance authorities they need. For those who believe executive branch officials will voluntarily interpret their surveillance authorities with restraint, I believe it is more likely that I will achieve my life-long dream of playing in the NBA.

The Definition of Tyranny

But seriously, when James Madison was attempting to persuade Americans that the Constitution contained sufficient protections against any politician or bureaucrat seizing more power than that granted to them by the people, he did not just ask his fellow Americans to trust him. He carefully laid out the protections contained in the Constitution and how the people could ensure they were not breached. We are failing our constituents, we are failing our founders, and we are failing every brave man and woman who fought to protect American democracy if we are willing, today, to just trust any individual or any agency with power greater than the checked and limited authority that serves as a firewall against tyranny. . . .

We find ourselves at a truly unique time in our Constitutional history. The growth of digital technology, dramatic changes in the nature of warfare and the definition of a battlefield, and novel courts that run counter to everything the Founding Fathers imagined, make for a combustible mix. At this point in the speech I would usually conclude with the quote from Ben Franklin about giving up liberty for security and not deserving either, but I thought a different founding father might be more fitting today. James Madison, the father of our Constitution, said that the the accumulation of executive, judicial and legislative powers into the hands of any faction is the very definition of tyranny. He then went on to assure the nation that the Constitution protected us from that fate. So, my question to you is: by allowing the executive to secretly follow a secret interpretation of the law under the supervision of a secret, non-adversarial court and occasional secret congressional hearings, how close are we coming to James Madison's "very definition of tyranny"? I believe we are allowing our country to drift a lot closer than we should, and if we don't take this opportunity to change course now, we will all live to regret it.

The US Government Should Stop Mass Data Collection

Ken Gude

Ken Gude is a senior fellow with the National Security Team at the Center for American Progress.

President Barack Obama will deliver a major speech tomorrow [January 17, 2014] regarding the National Security Agency's, or NSA's, intelligence collection activities, both in the United States and around the world. There has been great controversy and confusion around these activities since former NSA contractor Edward Snowden began leaking details of these and other NSA programs last June. Many Americans were particularly shocked by the revelation that the government maintained a secret database of all the telephone calls made by or to phones in the United States. The existence of government data collection on this scale could influence the choices Americans make with profound negative effects on our society and economy.

A new report from President Obama's handpicked review panel to examine the NSA programs has provided some clarity about the different NSA collection programs and focused the debate on whether such bulk collection should continue. The president has the authority right now to suspend this bulk collection and instead require the NSA to seek an order from the court that oversees this activity each time it wants to search phone records. Doing so in this manner would not harm national security but would get the government out of the mass data collection business and re-establish meaningful checks on the NSA when searching Americans' phone records.

How the Bulk Collection Program Works

Currently, the U.S. Foreign Intelligence Surveillance Court, or FISA Court, authorizes the NSA under Section 215 of the USA PATRIOT Act, or Patriot Act, to collect the metadata from multiple phone companies on all telephone calls made within, to, or from the United States and consolidate it into a massive database stretching back over five years of call records. The NSA then decides when and on whom to make queries of this metadata database based on the reasonable articulable suspicion, or RAS, that the target of the search is connected to international terrorism.

The specter of mass collection is the problem, along with its potential impact on the choices of Americans in the global information age.

After the NSA analyzes the target's call records, it can then make two more searches, or hops, of the database looking for connections that can identify terrorist networks. If the average person calls or is called by 100 different numbers over a five-year period—the so-called first hop—and each of those numbers is also connected to 100 other numbers and so forth, the second hop would return a search of 10,000 numbers, and the third hop would return 1,000,000. So one seed number can allow the NSA to search the records of 1,000,000 Americans.

The FISA Court's current oversight is at the programmatic level—the authorizing of bulk collection—and of minimal utility because it does not scrutinize in advance the NSA's decisions to hop to 1 million call records. In now-public rulings, however, we know the FISA Court repeatedly held that the NSA exceeded court-imposed limits on these searches. It is true that stronger procedures are now in place at the NSA to prevent its searches from intentionally or unintentionally exceeding these court-imposed limits. And it is appropriate to believe the good-faith arguments of the responsible NSA officials that their only intention is to protect Americans from attack by lawful means, as well as that the NSA will report to the FISA Court any action that exceeds its lawful authority. Yet this self-policing is insufficient given the depth of the American public's mistrust of the NSA and the American system of government that is based on meaningful checks on any such activity.

The Fear of a Chilling Effect

In addition to concerns about viable oversight of the program as currently constructed, a greater fear is the potential, chilling effect that could result from the existence of a huge government database containing all the telephone-call records of all Americans. The specter of mass collection is the problem, along with its potential impact on the choices of Americans in the global information age.

Modern communications technologies have dramatically improved Americans' ability to stay connected with one another. Other modern information technology has provided greater access to more information for more people than ever before, and it has significantly lowered the barriers to participation in public discussion and debate. As a result, our country is undergoing an information revolution that is driving the kind of innovation that will protect America's global economic leadership. Although this transformation has not come without costs, it has enormously benefited American democracy, our economy, and our global competitiveness.

At the same time, these new technologies create huge amounts of unique data about the daily activities and beliefs of millions of Americans. Regardless of whether the information is freely turned over to third parties by the traditional legal definition established by the Supreme Court in the days of rotary telephones and before personal computing, it is simply not possible to actively participate in American society today without leaving a digital trail from which a detailed picture of one's life can be drawn. Who you talk to, what you read, what you buy, and who you consider friends are all easily and precisely found in our modern digital world.

President Obama should immediately suspend bulk metadata collection under Section 215 of the Patriot Act and instead require the NSA to obtain an order from the FISA Court for each specific query.

The reality of the telephone metadata program on its own clearly does not sweep in all of our digital data. This is not the only such collection program, however, and the NSA's Internet metadata program was suspended at the end of 2011 only because of excessive cost, not due to an NSA judgment that the program violated legal limits. Regardless, the government being in the mass digital data collection business at all is the problem. Furthermore, it does not require a conspiratorial mind to be concerned about what other programs are out there when a secret government database of all the call records of all Americans has existed for nearly a decade. It would prove extremely damaging to our society if Americans began to feel they needed to choose between fully participating in American public and economic life and their right to keep the intimate details of their core activities and beliefs out of the hands of the government.

A Proposed Change

In somewhat of a surprise, the president's intelligence review panel recommended significant changes to the bulk collection program. It favored new legislation that would end the NSA's bulk collection and instead leave the call-record data in the hands of the telephone companies or, if that was deemed too difficult to manage, establish a third party to hold a consolidated database. This would be a meaningful change and would allow the FISA Court to check the NSA's actions when the agency collects and searches Americans' telephone records. Having Congress engage on this critical issue is also important, as it has been excluded from consideration of it until now.

Congress reauthorized Section 215 of the Patriot Act in 2006, and, shortly after it became law, the [George W.] Bush administration argued in secret to the FISA Court that the section was extremely broad and allowed bulk metadata collection. The FISA Court agreed and issued a secret ruling that approved such power. At no point during this consideration of the Patriot Act reauthorization did Congress debate whether Section 215 would authorize bulk collection of metadata. Congress reauthorized this section of the Patriot Act in 2010 and 2011 without change. There was no public debate, Congress was never provided with the legal reasoning that supported this expansive interpretation of Section 215, most members of Congress had no idea that this was how the law was being applied, and those that did were specifically prohibited from making any public statement about it. Having Congress provide its view on this program is essential, but let's be clear: It would be the first time Congress has been allowed to make an informed judgment on it.

Consequently, President Obama should immediately suspend bulk metadata collection under Section 215 of the Patriot Act and instead require the NSA to obtain an order from the FISA Court for each specific query. The NSA could secure individual orders under Section 215 for call records pertaining to any identifier that meets their current RAS standard, and each order would cover current telephone metadata records residing with the phone companies and those in the existing database of such records.

The president should also request that the phone companies ensure that they preserve these call-record data in a similar format to how they are currently transmitted to the NSA for a period of at least 18 months. Current federal regulations require the phone companies to store these data for 18 months for accuracy in billing, and the president should make clear that the phone companies must preserve the records in a format that allows the companies to be quickly responsive to FISA Court orders. This would give Congress and the president ample time to create through legislation a nonprofit third-party entity to serve as the repository of a consolidated database of records from multiple companies. This would get the government out of the data collection business and provide meaningful distance from the program for telephone companies so as not to harm their business by the specter of association with mass data collection.

In the event that there is a small disruption of the [NSA surveillance] program because of this change, however unlikely, it is an acceptable tradeoff to get the government out of the mass collection business.

Suspending bulk collection in this manner preserves the NSA's capability to access metadata for counterterrorism purposes while Congress and the president work out new legislation, and, therefore, it does not harm national security. Taking this decisive action would also establish a clear and strong position for the president with the American people and help restore their trust that the government is not in the mass collection business.

Concerns Regarding This Change

Critics of this change claim that extra time would be required to consolidate data from multiple phone companies into the format that is searchable by NSA systems using an RAS query. While the technical details of the current NSA bulk collection program remain appropriately classified, it is clear that the NSA already possesses the capability to convert the metadata it receives from different telephone companies into a format compatible with its supercomputers and algorithms. Otherwise, the NSA would not be able to operate the program as currently constructed. As a matter of logic, the time required to collect and convert an individual's—or even several individuals'—metadata into the compatible format would be no more than that required under the current program with millions of records.

In the event that there is a small disruption of the program because of this change, however unlikely, it is an acceptable tradeoff to get the government out of the mass collection business. Additionally, given its mission and resources, the NSA should be able to adapt its systems to meet these new requirements and eliminate any delays that arise during the transition period if so ordered by the president.

Another concern is that in an emergency, the added time of both technical hurdles and the necessity to obtain an order from the FISA Court could undermine the capability to prevent terrorist attacks. The telephone metadata program may be useful in a scenario in which the government needs to determine as quickly as possible whether a terrorist attacker has connections to others inside the United States. This change, however, should not diminish that capability. In the current system with rolling bulk collection, whatever time is required to convert the bulk metadata into the format used by the NSA establishes a window of call records for any target that cannot be searched immediately. As noted above, it could not possibly take the NSA any longer to convert a handful of records than it does for the current millions of records; therefore, that window would not be larger for technical reasons under this proposed change.

Obtaining approval from the FISA Court and serving orders on the telephone companies in such an emergency would add additional steps but not significant additional time. The FISA Court can approve orders in the small hours of the night on an emergency basis, and procedures for immediate notification and response by the telephone companies can be established in advance if they do not already exist. And the government has many different tools, such as wiretaps, to obtain information about any telephone use from known and still-at-large terrorists as quickly as possible.

Ending the practice of mass digital data collection by the government is essential as we navigate our way into the global information age. Requiring the NSA to seek individual orders to search Americans' telephone-call records in a database not controlled by the government would maintain the capability to use this information for legitimate counterterrorism purposes. Conversely, preserving a government-held database of such a large scale approved by an informed Congress would establish an enduring legal framework of mass digital data collection by the government that could impact the way Americans choose to live their lives with negative effects on our democracy and our economy.

It's time to get the government out of the mass data collection business.

Legislation Allowing Mass Data Collection Should Not Be Weakened

Fred Fleitz and Clare Lopez

Fred Fleitz is senior vice president and Clare Lopez is vice president for research and analysis at the Center for Security Policy.

We agree with the [President's] Review Group [on Intelligence and Communications Technologies] that steps need to be taken to reassure the American people about the legality of the Patriot Act Section 215 and related programs and that they are not a threat to privacy. However, the Group's recommendations would seriously weaken the program's effectiveness and would create real privacy concerns by having private parties—in addition to telephone companies—hold telephone metadata of Americans instead of NSA [National Security Agency].

We believe the best way to address concerns about the 215 program is through bipartisan legislation under discussion in the congressional intelligence committees. The Senate Select Intelligence Committee (SSCI) attempted to do this when it passed the FISA Improvements Act of 2013 by a decisive vote of 11 to 4 last October [2013]. The House Intelligence Committee reportedly is working on a similar bill. The SSCI bill would codify a requirement for NSA analysts to have a "reasonable articulable suspicion" that a phone number is associated with terrorism to query the metadata database. The bill would also impose a five-year limit on the retention of bulk communication records acquired under Section 215 of the Pa-

Fred Fleitz and Clare Lopez, "A Critique of the Recommendations by the President's Review Group on Intelligence and Communications Technologies," Center for Security Policy, January 13, 2014, pp. 1–3. © Center for Security Policy. All Rights Reserved. Reproduced by permission.

triot Act and require Attorney General approval to query records that are older than three years. It calls for closer review by the FISA court and additional annual reports to the committee on 215 queries.

The constitutionality of the 215 program ... has been upheld through 36 challenges before 16 different judges.

We believe the FISA Improvements Act is a step in the right direction and should become the basis of a House-Senate bill addressed to the 215 program. We ask the President to work with the congressional intelligence committees on new legislation to bolster the 215 program and not adopt the Review Panel's recommendations.

The Review Group's Recommendations

The first 11 recommendations and Recommendation 20 in the Review Group report address the principal reason for its report: NSA collection of telephone metadata records as authorized under Section 215 of the Patriot Act which allows NSA to hold and search these phone records to find intelligence on terrorist-related connections. Leaks about the 215 program by Edward Snowden have caused a firestorm of criticism that it violates the privacy rights of Americans and allows NSA to monitor their personal phone calls. In fact, this program does not allow the government to monitor phone calls, only phone records which several judges have concluded are not subject to privacy protections. *While the Review Group would keep the 215 program in place, we oppose all of its recommendations on this program as they would place so many limitations on the metadata program that it would be rendered virtually useless. We also believe these recommendations address privacy concerns that lack validity and would actually increase the potential for real privacy violations.*

U.S. District Judge for the District of Columbia Richard Leon was highly critical of the 215 program in his December 16 [2013] decision *Klayman vs Obama,* writing that it is probably a violation of the Fourth Amendment. In a December 27 decision, *ACLU vs Clapper,* Southern District of New York Judge William H. Pauley came to the opposite conclusion, ruling that the 215 effort is a lawful and vital counterterrorism intelligence program which he described as the government's "counterpunch connecting fragmented and fleeting communications to reconstruct and eliminate al-Qaeda's terror network."

The constitutionality of the 215 program is based on the 1979 Supreme Court case *Smith vs Maryland* and has been upheld through 36 challenges before 16 different judges. The review panel questions whether the Smith decision is still good law. We believe it is and that the Supreme Court is likely to uphold 215 based on this decision when it ultimately rules on appeals of the *Klayman* and *ACLU* decisions.

Allegations have been made that this program is overly broad, gives NSA too much discretion as to how and when to employ it, and has been subject to insufficient oversight by the Foreign Surveillance Intelligence Court (FISC) and the congressional intelligence committees. However, the Review Group, Judge Leon and Judge Pauley all agree that there is no evidence that the 215 program has been abused.

The recommendations of the Review Group are not based on abuses or malfeasance. They are based on theoretical abuses of this program.

The Value of the Metadata Program

Although the Review Group report states that the 215 program "was not essential to preventing terrorist attacks," Review Group member Michael Morell contradicted this finding just after the report was issued when he said in a December 27, 2013 *Washington Post* op-ed that if the metadata program had been in place before September 2001, "it would likely have prevented 9/11" and "has the potential to prevent the next 9/11."

Another significant endorsement of the 215 program came from a bipartisan statement on December 20, 2013 by the top four members of the House and Senate intelligence committees in which they strongly disagreed with the panel's recommendations. This letter said:

> "The NSA's metadata program is a valuable analytical tool that assists intelligence personnel in their efforts to efficiently 'connect the dots' on emerging or current terrorist threats directed against Americans in the United States. The necessity of this program cannot be measured merely by the number of terrorist attacks disrupted, but must also take into account the extent to which it contributes to the overall efforts of intelligence professionals to quickly respond to, and prevent, rapidly emerging terrorist threats."

We believe this bipartisan statement by members of Congress who understand the metadata program and have closely overseen it for several years should guide President [Barack] Obama's decision on any steps he chooses to reform it.

The recommendations of the Review Group are not based on abuses or malfeasance. They are based on theoretical abuses of this program, such as gathering metadata to cull personal information like medical records. There is no indication that such an abuse has ever been contemplated, much less carried out. Moreover, the 22 people who have access to the metadata database are closely monitored and forbidden to use it in any fashion other than against suspect telephone numbers.

The most troubling rationale offered by the Review Group for these and other recommendations is to recommend dramatic changes because the potential for abuse "can significantly undermine public trust." That reasoning can be applied to any intelligence program, and indeed to any law enforcement activity: the police officer could beat an innocent citizen with his nightstick, or shoot such a citizen with his pistol; that is not an argument in favor of confiscating police nightsticks or pistols. Indeed, the Review Group concedes, even as it fails to appreciate, that "the degree of oversight and control by high-level officials, legislative members and the judiciary" makes U.S. intelligence collection "unique."

Opposition to the Recommendations

The Review Group makes 12 recommendations which we believe would weaken the 215 program.

Recommendations 1 to 4 would place severe limitations on the issuance of 215 orders and National Security letters. *We oppose these recommendations because we regard them as unwarranted steps that would create new legal obstacles to quickly obtaining Section 215 orders to address urgent national security threats, especially potential terrorist attacks.*

Recommendations 4 and 5 would bar the government from collecting and holding metadata and call for a new system under which metadata would instead be held either by private providers or by a private third party. *We oppose these recommendations because they would create major obstacles to NSA obtaining quick access to the full range of data needed for this program to be effective. We also believe that allowing private parties to hold this data raises the real possibility of increased privacy and national security risks since this information would be kept on less secure servers in numerous locations. A much larger set of people would need to manage this data and would not be subject to NSA's clearance procedures. This would increase new security and privacy vulnerabilities.*

New Technologies Should Not Hinder Law Enforcement Surveillance

James B. Comey

James B. Comey is director of the US Federal Bureau of Investigation (FBI).

Technology has forever changed the world we live in. We're online, in one way or another, all day long. Our phones and computers have become reflections of our personalities, our interests, and our identities. They hold much that is important to us.

And with that comes a desire to protect our privacy and our data—you want to share your lives with the people you choose. I sure do. But the FBI [Federal Bureau of Investigation] has a sworn duty to keep every American safe from crime and terrorism, and technology has become the tool of choice for some very dangerous people.

Unfortunately, the law hasn't kept pace with technology, and this disconnect has created a significant public safety problem. We call it "Going Dark," and what it means is this: Those charged with protecting our people aren't always able to access the evidence we need to prosecute crime and prevent terrorism even with lawful authority. We have the legal authority to intercept and access communications and information pursuant to court order, but we often lack the technical ability to do so.

Conducting Legal Interception

We face two overlapping challenges. The first concerns real-time court-ordered interception of what we call "data in mo-

James B. Comey, "Going Dark: Are Technology, Privacy, and Public Safety on a Collision Course?" Speech at the Brookings Institution, October 16, 2014. © FBI - Federal Bureau Of Investigation. All Rights Reserved. Reproduced by permission.

tion," such as phone calls, e-mail, and live chat sessions. The second challenge concerns court-ordered access to data stored on our devices, such as e-mail, text messages, photos, and videos—or what we call "data at rest." And both real-time communication and stored data are increasingly encrypted.

If a suspected criminal is in his car, and he switches from cellular coverage to Wi-Fi, we may be out of luck.

Let's talk about court-ordered interception first, and then we'll talk about challenges posed by different means of encryption.

In the past, conducting electronic surveillance was more straightforward. We identified a target phone being used by a bad guy, with a single carrier. We obtained a court order for a wiretap, and, under the supervision of a judge, we collected the evidence we needed for prosecution.

Today, there are countless providers, countless networks, and countless means of communicating. We have laptops, smartphones, and tablets. We take them to work and to school, from the soccer field to Starbucks, over many networks, using any number of apps. And so do those conspiring to harm us. They use the same devices, the same networks, and the same apps to make plans, to target victims, and to cover up what they're doing. And that makes it tough for us to keep up.

If a suspected criminal is in his car, and he switches from cellular coverage to Wi-Fi, we may be out of luck. If he switches from one app to another, or from cellular voice service to a voice or messaging app, we may lose him. We may not have the capability to quickly switch lawful surveillance between devices, methods, and networks. The bad guys know this; they're taking advantage of it every day.

In the wake of the [Edward] Snowden disclosures, the prevailing view is that the government is sweeping up all of our communications. That is not true. And unfortunately, the idea that the government has access to all communications at all times has extended—unfairly—to the investigations of law enforcement agencies that obtain individual warrants, approved by judges, to intercept the communications of suspected criminals.

The Challenge of New Technology

Some believe that the FBI has these phenomenal capabilities to access any information at any time—that we can get what we want, when we want it, by flipping some sort of switch. It may be true in the movies or on TV. It is simply not the case in real life.

It frustrates me, because I want people to understand that law enforcement needs to be able to access communications and information to bring people to justice. We do so pursuant to the rule of law, with clear guidance and strict oversight. But even with lawful authority, we may not be able to access the evidence and the information we need.

The challenge to law enforcement and national security officials is markedly worse, with recent default encryption settings and encrypted devices and networks—all designed to increase security and privacy.

Current law governing the interception of communications requires telecommunication carriers and broadband providers to build interception capabilities into their networks for court-ordered surveillance. But that law, the Communications Assistance for Law Enforcement Act, or CALEA, was enacted 20 years ago—a lifetime in the Internet age. And it doesn't cover new means of communication. Thousands of companies provide some form of communication service, and most are not required by statute to provide lawful intercept capabilities to law enforcement.

What this means is that an order from a judge to monitor a suspect's communication may amount to nothing more than a piece of paper. Some companies fail to comply with the court order. Some can't comply, because they have not developed interception capabilities. Other providers want to provide assistance, but they have to build interception capabilities, and that takes time and money.

The issue is whether companies not currently subject to the Communications Assistance for Law Enforcement Act should be required to build lawful intercept capabilities for law enforcement. We aren't seeking to expand our authority to intercept communications. We are struggling to keep up with changing technology and to maintain our ability to actually collect the communications we are authorized to intercept.

And if the challenges of real-time interception threaten to leave us in the dark, encryption threatens to lead all of us to a very dark place.

The Challenge of Encryption

Encryption is nothing new. But the challenge to law enforcement and national security officials is markedly worse, with recent default encryption settings and encrypted devices and networks—all designed to increase security and privacy.

With Apple's new operating system, the information stored on many iPhones and other Apple devices will be encrypted by default. Shortly after Apple's announcement, Google announced plans to follow suit with its Android operating system. This means the companies themselves won't be able to unlock phones, laptops, and tablets to reveal photos, documents, e-mail, and recordings stored within.

Both companies are run by good people, responding to what they perceive is a market demand. But the place they are leading us is one we shouldn't go to without careful thought and debate as a country.

At the outset, Apple says something that is reasonable—that it's not that big a deal. Apple argues, for example, that its users can back-up and store much of their data in "the cloud" and that the FBI can still access that data with lawful authority. But uploading to the cloud doesn't include all of the stored data on a bad guy's phone, which has the potential to create a black hole for law enforcement.

And if the bad guys don't back up their phones routinely, or if they opt out of uploading to the cloud, the data will only be found on the encrypted devices themselves. And it is people most worried about what's on the phone who will be most likely to avoid the cloud and to make sure that law enforcement cannot access incriminating data.

Encryption isn't just a technical feature; it's a marketing pitch. But it will have very serious consequences for law enforcement and national security agencies at all levels. Sophisticated criminals will come to count on these means of evading detection. It's the equivalent of a closet that can't be opened. A safe that can't be cracked. And my question is, at what cost?

With sophisticated encryption, there might be no solution, leaving the government at a dead end—all in the name of privacy and network security.

The Need for a Lawful Intercept Solution

Some argue that we will still have access to metadata, which includes telephone records and location information from telecommunications carriers. That is true. But metadata doesn't provide the content of any communication. It's incomplete information, and even this is difficult to access when time is of the essence. I wish we had time in our work, especially when lives are on the line. We usually don't.

There is a misconception that building a lawful intercept solution into a system requires a so-called "back door," one that foreign adversaries and hackers may try to exploit.

But that isn't true. We aren't seeking a back-door approach. We want to use the front door, with clarity and transparency, and with clear guidance provided by law. We are completely comfortable with court orders and legal process—front doors that provide the evidence and information we need to investigate crime and prevent terrorist attacks.

Cyber adversaries will exploit any vulnerability they find. But it makes more sense to address any security risks by developing intercept solutions during the design phase, rather than resorting to a patchwork solution when law enforcement comes knocking after the fact. And with sophisticated encryption, there might be no solution, leaving the government at a dead end—all in the name of privacy and network security.

Another misperception is that we can somehow guess the password or break into the phone with a so-called "brute force" attack. Even a supercomputer would have difficulty with today's high-level encryption, and some devices have a setting whereby the encryption key is erased if someone makes too many attempts to break the password, meaning no one can access that data.

What Criminals Want

Finally, a reasonable person might also ask, "Can't you just compel the owner of the phone to produce the password?" Likely, no. And even if we could compel them as a legal matter, if we had a child predator in custody, and he could choose to sit quietly through a 30-day contempt sentence for refusing to comply with a court order to produce his password, or he could risk a 30-year sentence for production and distribution of child pornography, which do you think he would choose?

Think about life without your smartphone, without Internet access, without texting or e-mail or the apps you use every day. I'm guessing most of you would feel rather lost and left behind. Kids call this FOMO, or "fear of missing out."

With Going Dark, those of us in law enforcement and public safety have a major fear of missing out—missing out on predators who exploit the most vulnerable among us . . . missing out on violent criminals who target our communities . . . missing out on a terrorist cell using social media to recruit, plan, and execute an attack.

Criminals and terrorists would like nothing more than for us to miss out. And the more we as a society rely on these devices, the more important they are to law enforcement and public safety officials. We have seen case after case—from homicides and car crashes to drug trafficking, domestic abuse, and child exploitation—where critical evidence came from smartphones, hard drives, and online communication. . . .

The Rule of Law

I'm deeply concerned about this, as both a law enforcement officer and a citizen. I understand some of this thinking in a post-Snowden world, but I believe it is mostly based on a failure to understand why we in law enforcement do what we do and how we do it.

There will come a day . . . where it will matter a great deal to innocent people that we in law enforcement can't access certain types of data or information, even with legal authorization.

I hope you know that I'm a huge believer in the rule of law. But I also believe that no one in this country should be above or beyond the law. There should be no law-free zone in this country. I like and believe very much that we need to follow the letter of the law to examine the contents of someone's closet or someone's cell phone. But the notion that the marketplace could create something that would prevent that closet from ever being opened, even with a properly obtained court order, makes no sense to me.

I think it's time to ask: Where are we, as a society? Are we no longer a country governed by the rule of law, where no one is above or beyond that law? Are we so mistrustful of government—and of law enforcement—that we are willing to let bad guys walk away . . . willing to leave victims in search of justice?

There will come a day—and it comes every day in this business—where it will matter a great deal to innocent people that we in law enforcement can't access certain types of data or information, even with legal authorization. We have to have these discussions now.

The Distrust of Government

I believe people should be skeptical of government power. I am. This country was founded by people who were worried about government power—who knew that you cannot trust people in power. So they divided government power among three branches, with checks and balances for each. And they wrote a Bill of Rights to ensure that the "papers and effects" of the people are secure from unreasonable searches.

But the way I see it, the means by which we conduct surveillance through telecommunication carriers and those Internet service providers who have developed lawful intercept solutions is an example of government operating in the way the founders intended—that is, the executive, the legislative, and the judicial branches proposing, enacting, executing, and overseeing legislation, pursuant to the rule of law.

Perhaps it's time to suggest that the post-Snowden pendulum has swung too far in one direction—in a direction of fear and mistrust. It is time to have open and honest debates about liberty and security.

Some have suggested there is a conflict between liberty and security. I disagree. At our best, we in law enforcement, national security, and public safety are looking for security that enhances liberty. When a city posts police officers at a dangerous playground, security has promoted liberty—the freedom to let a child play without fear.

The people of the FBI are sworn to protect both security and liberty. It isn't a question of conflict. We must care deeply about protecting liberty through due process of law, while also safeguarding the citizens we serve—in every investigation.

The Need for Balance

These are tough issues. And finding the space and time in our busy lives to understand these issues is hard. Intelligent people can and do disagree, and that's the beauty of American life— that smart people can come to the right answer.

We need assistance and cooperation from companies to comply with lawful court orders, so that criminals around the world cannot seek safe haven for lawless conduct.

I've never been someone who is a scaremonger. But I'm in a dangerous business. So I want to ensure that when we discuss limiting the court-authorized law enforcement tools we use to investigate suspected criminals that we understand what society gains and what we all stand to lose.

We in the FBI will continue to throw every lawful tool we have at this problem, but it's costly. It's inefficient. And it takes time.

We need to fix this problem. It is long past time.

We need assistance and cooperation from companies to comply with lawful court orders, so that criminals around the world cannot seek safe haven for lawless conduct. We need to find common ground. We care about the same things. I said it because I meant it. These companies are run by good people. And we know an adversarial posture won't take any of us very far down the road.

We understand the private sector's need to remain competitive in the global marketplace. And it isn't our intent to stifle innovation or undermine U.S. companies. But we have to find a way to help these companies understand what we need, why we need it, and how they can help, while still protecting privacy rights and providing network security and innovation. We need our private sector partners to take a step back, to pause, and to consider changing course.

We also need a regulatory or legislative fix to create a level playing field, so that all communication service providers are held to the same standard and so that those of us in law enforcement, national security, and public safety can continue to do the job you have entrusted us to do, in the way you would want us to.

Perhaps most importantly, we need to make sure the American public understands the work we do and the means by which we do it.

I really do believe we can get there, with a reasoned and practical approach. And we have to get there together. I don't have the perfect solution. But I think it's important to start the discussion. I'm happy to work with Congress, with our partners in the private sector, with my law enforcement and national security counterparts, and with the people we serve, to find the right answer—to find the balance we need.

New Technologies Should Not Facilitate Government Surveillance

Center for Democracy and Technology

The Center for Democracy and Technology is a nonprofit organization whose mission is to promote an open, innovative, and free Internet.

Encrypting smartphones and other tech products will help protect against malicious hacking, identity theft, phone theft, and other crimes. However, a government mandate requiring companies to build a "backdoor" through encryption to facilitate surveillance would put consumers at grave risk and impose heavy costs on US businesses. The government can obtain information for investigations from other sources, and may be able to compel an individual to decrypt information with a search warrant.

The Change to Encryption

Apple and Google recently announced that their newer smartphones will be "encrypted by default." This means that all the data stored on the phone itself will be unreadable to anyone who accesses the phone without knowing the owner's password or key to unlock the encryption. Weak encryption (or obvious passwords) can be broken by widely available cracking programs, but Apple and Google announced they will apply strong encryption to their devices. Prior to this announcement, many other companies and nonprofits have long offered products and services, including phones, secured by strong encryption to the public.

The primary impact of this change will be to increase security from cybercriminals for regular smartphone users. Encryption by default ensures that if criminals steal or attempt to hack into a phone, they will be unable to access the owner's sensitive data stored on the device, such as credit card information, photos, emails, medical records, social media accounts, and more. Millions of American smartphone users are targets of identity theft, phone theft, and cybercrime, and the principle objective of securing smartphones with strong encryption is to protect against these problems.

A government-mandated security vulnerability in tech products would ... be a huge burden on businesses and an obstacle to innovation.

The FBI [Federal Bureau of Investigation] wants a "backdoor" into encrypted products—not just phones, but other communications services as well. In a recent speech, FBI Director [James B.] Comey called for companies to build security flaws into their encrypted products so that the government can break through and wiretap consumers or seize data stored on their devices. Director Comey suggested that Congress should enact legislation to impose this requirement on "all communications service providers."

During his speech, Director Comey stated the FBI was not actually seeking a backdoor because he is proposing that companies intentionally build a means of breaking encryption for the purpose of government access into their products and services. However, this conflates a legal backdoor with a technical one: as a technical matter, creating a path through encryption to provide access that the user does not authorize is, by definition, a "backdoor" security vulnerability into the device. It is impossible to build encryption that can be circumvented without creating a technical backdoor.

The Problem with Backdoors

Backdoors severely weaken cybersecurity, leaving users exposed to malicious hacking and crime. A government-mandated security vulnerability in tech products would also be a huge burden on businesses and an obstacle to innovation.

A fundamental problem with a backdoor is that there is no way to control who goes through it. If the US government can exploit a backdoor security vulnerability to access a consumer's device, so will malicious hackers, identity thieves, and foreign governments. This will devastate the security of not just individual consumers around the world, but also the many businesses that use American commercial tech products day-to-day. Ultimately, this mandate would have the effect of actually enabling cybercrime and undermining national security.

Consumers outside of the US may be much less inclined to purchase American tech products that facilitate government surveillance. Consider, for example, the difficulty US companies would have selling smartphones or network servers in the EU that are built to enable easy access for the NSA [National Security Agency]. As a technical matter, it is difficult and expensive to both build a backdoor security vulnerability and then defend that vulnerability against unauthorized use. This burden would be heaviest on small businesses and innovators of new communications services, which may create a disincentive to encrypt their products and services, which would reduce the overall security of users.

There is no doubt that some communications are more difficult to intercept than others, and that the FBI has a legitimate concern that criminals and terrorists will gravitate to communications technologies that are more difficult to surveil. However, taken as a whole, the digital revolution has made more data about us available than ever before, and the government has more tools to obtain and analyze that data than ever before. The volume of government surveillance increases almost every year. The claim that companies' increasing adoption of strong encryption by default will suddenly lead to government "going dark" and unable to access critical information is speculative.

If information is encrypted in one place, it is often available from another source.

Products and software with strong encryption have been freely available to the public—including criminals—for many years, and have not rendered law enforcement helpless to investigate crimes. By recently choosing to encrypt popular smartphones by default, companies are making this security feature easier to use and more accessible to regular smartphone users who do not seek out increased security protection. This change will *reduce* overall crime by protecting all smartphone users, rather than just those who are already security-conscious.

The Debate About Decryption

The government has not yet produced an actual case in which decrypting a device was essential to attaining a conviction. In his recent speech, Director Comey cited several terrible crimes where cell phone evidence came into play, but in every one of these cases the evidence on the phone was not critical to the conviction and the government had other ways of obtaining the data it sought. When a reporter asked Director Comey for a real-life instance when ability to access data on a phone was critical to rescuing an individual, he responded, "I haven't found one yet" despite canvassing state and local law enforcement for examples.

If information is encrypted in one place, it is often available from another source. For example, emails or text messages on an encrypted phone can be retrieved from the email service provider or the phone company. Many smartphones are backed up to the cloud, where the data can be obtained from the service provider through legal process. In addition, law enforcement may be able to compel a suspect to decrypt information or devices with a search warrant.

The Department of Justice takes the stance that the government can compel the owner of encrypted devices or account, such as a phone or an email account, to decrypt the information it seeks. The government has successfully argued in a number of cases that a warrant permits it to compel decryption. Whether compelled decryption is permissible or is barred by the Fifth Amendment hinges on a range of issues, including whether decryption is "testimonial," whether the existence of the information sought by the government is a "foregone conclusion," and whether immunity for the act of decryption is provided.

If an individual refuses an order to decrypt an electronic device, she could be held in contempt of court. When suspects refuse to testify or answer questions, courts can impose coercive and punitive punishments for contempt, including fines and imprisonment. Imprisonment for civil contempt can last for years, or until the order is obeyed. For example, the Third Circuit approved a contempt sentence that lasted 14 years, maintaining that individuals can be confined as long as they refuse a court order they are capable of obeying.

Organizations to Contact

The editors have compiled the following list of organizations concerned with the issues debated in this book. The descriptions are derived from materials provided by the organizations. All have publications or information available for interested readers. The list was compiled on the date of publication of the present volume; the information provided here may change. Be aware that many organizations take several weeks or longer to respond to inquiries, so allow as much time as possible.

American Civil Liberties Union (ACLU)
125 Broad St., 18th Floor, New York, NY   10004
(212) 549-2500
e-mail: infoaclu@aclu.org
website: www.aclu.org

The American Civil Liberties Union (ACLU) is a national organization that works to defend Americans' civil rights as guaranteed in the US Constitution. The ACLU works in courts, legislatures, and communities to defend First Amendment rights, the right to equal protection, the right to due process, and the right to privacy. The ACLU publishes the semiannual newsletter *Civil Liberties Alert*, as well as numerous briefings and reports, including "Surveillance Under the Patriot Act."

Brookings Institution
1775 Massachusetts Ave. NW, Washington, DC   20036
(202) 797-6000
e-mail: communications@brookings.edu
website: www.brookings.edu

The Brookings Institution is a nonprofit public policy organization that conducts independent research. The Brookings Institution uses its research to provide recommendations that advance the goals of strengthening American democracy, fostering social welfare and security, and securing a cooperative international system. The organization publishes a variety of books, reports, and commentary that deal with the issue of domestic surveillance.

Cato Institute
1000 Massachusetts Ave. NW, Washington, DC   20001-5403
(202) 842-0200 • fax: (202) 842-3490
website: www.cato.org

The Cato Institute is a public policy research organization dedicated to the principles of individual liberty, limited government, free markets, and peace. The Cato Institute aims to provide clear, thoughtful, and independent analysis on vital public policy issues. The Institute publishes numerous policy studies, two quarterly journals—*Regulation* and *Cato Journal*—and the bimonthly *Cato Policy Report*.

Center for Constitutional Rights (CCR)
666 Broadway, 7th Floor, New York, NY   10012
(212) 614-6464 • fax: (212) 614-6499
website: www.ccrjustice.org

The Center for Constitutional Rights (CCR) is a nonprofit legal and educational organization committed to the creative use of law as a positive force for social change. CCR is dedicated to advancing and protecting the rights guaranteed by the United States Constitution and the United Nations Universal Declaration of Human Rights. CCR publishes fact sheets and reports on the topics of constitutional rights, including surveillance and attacks on dissent.

Center for Democracy & Technology (CDT)
1634 I St. NW, #1100, Washington, DC   20006
(202) 637-9800 • fax: (202) 637-0968
website: www.cdt.org

The Center for Democracy & Technology (CDT) is a nonprofit organization that supports a user-controlled Internet and freedom of expression. CDT supports laws, corporate policies, and technology tools that protect the privacy of Internet users, and it advocates for stronger legal controls on government surveillance. At its website, the CDT provides numerous papers and a blog on issues regarding the Internet and surveillance.

Center for National Security Studies (CNSS)
1730 Pennsylvania Ave. NW, 7th Floor
Washington, DC 20006
(202) 721-5650 • fax: (202) 530-0128
e-mail: cnss@cnss.org
website: www.cnss.org

The Center for National Security Studies (CNSS) is an advocacy organization that serves as a watchdog in defense of civil liberties, human rights, and constitutional limits on government power. CNSS works to prevent illegal or unconstitutional government surveillance, combat excessive government secrecy and strengthen public access to information, and assure more effective oversight of intelligence agencies. The Center publishes a variety of statements, memos, legal briefs, letters, testimony, and speeches, all available at its website.

Center for Security Policy
1901 Pennsylvania Ave. NW, Suite 201
Washington, DC 20006
(202) 835-9077
e-mail: info@centerforsecuritypolicy.org
website: www.centerforsecuritypolicy.org

The Center for Security Policy is a nonprofit, nonpartisan, national security organization that works to establish successful national security policies through the use of diplomatic, informational, military, and economic strength. The Center believes that America's national power must be preserved and properly used because it holds a unique global role in maintaining peace and stability. The organization publishes periodic *Occasional Papers* and articles, all of which are available at its website.

Electronic Frontier Foundation (EFF)

454 Shotwell St., San Francisco, CA   94110-1914
(415) 436-9333 • fax: (415) 436-9993
e-mail: info@eff.org
website: www.eff.org

The Electronic Frontier Foundation (EFF) works to promote the public interest in critical battles affecting digital rights. EFF provides legal assistance in cases where it believes it can help shape the law. EFF publishes a newsletter and reports, including "NSA Surveillance: Demand Accountability."

Electronic Privacy Information Center (EPIC)

1718 Connecticut Ave. NW, Suite 200, Washington, DC   20009
(202) 483-1140 • fax: (202) 483-1248
website: www.epic.org

The Electronic Privacy Information Center (EPIC) is a public interest research center aimed at protecting privacy, the First Amendment, and constitutional values. EPIC engages in research aimed at focusing public attention on emerging civil liberties issues. EPIC publishes an online newsletter on civil liberties in the information age, the *EPIC Alert*.

National Security Agency (NSA)

9800 Savage Rd., Fort Meade, MD   20755-6248
(301) 688-6524
website: www.nsa.gov

The National Security Agency (NSA) provides information to US decision makers and military leaders. The NSA coordinates, directs, and performs activities that protect American information systems and produce foreign intelligence information. The NSA provides speeches, briefings, and reports on public information at its website.

Privacy International

62 Britton St., London   EC1M 5UY
  United Kingdom

(44) 20 3422 4321
e-mail: info@privacy.org
website: www.privacyinternational.org

Privacy International's mission is to defend the right to privacy across the world, and to fight surveillance and other intrusions into private life by governments and corporations. Privacy International works at national and international levels to ensure strong legal protections for privacy and seeks ways to protect privacy through the use of technology. Privacy International conducts research to raise awareness about threats to privacy and publishes reports on surveillance methods and tactics, such as "An Assessment of the EU-US Travel Surveillance Agreement."

Bibliography

Books

Julia Angwin

Dragnet Nation: A Quest for Privacy, Security, and Freedom in a World of Relentless Surveillance. New York: Times Books, Henry Holt and Company, 2014.

Heidi Boghosian

Spying on Democracy: Government Surveillance, Corporate Power and Public Resistance. San Francisco: City Lights, 2013.

Ronald J. Deibert

Black Code: Surveillance, Privacy, and the Dark Side of the Internet. Toronto: Signal, 2013.

John C. Domino

Civil Rights and Liberties in the 21st Century. New York: Longman, 2010.

Martin R. Dowding

Privacy: Defending an Illusion. Lanham, MD: Scarecrow Press, 2011.

A.C. Grayling

Liberty in the Age of Terror: A Defence of Civil Liberties and Enlightenment Values. New York: Bloomsbury, 2011.

Glenn Greenwald

No Place to Hide: Edward Snowden, the NSA, and the US Surveillance State. New York: Henry Holt and Company, 2014.

Luke Harding

The Snowden Files: The Inside Story of the World's Most Wanted Man. New York: Vintage, 2014.

Susan Landau   *Surveillance or Security? The Risks Posed by New Wiretapping Technologies.* Cambridge, MA: MIT Press, 2013.

Cynthia Lee, ed.   *The Fourth Amendment. Searches and Seizures: Its Constitutional History and Contemporary Debate.* Amherst, NY: Prometheus Books, 2011.

Evgeny Morozov   *The Net Delusion: The Dark Side of Internet Freedom.* New York: PublicAffairs, 2011.

Cath Senker   *Privacy and Surveillance.* New York: Rosen Central, 2012.

Robert H. Sloan and Richard Warner   *Unauthorized Access: The Crisis in Online Privacy and Security.* Boca Raton, FL: CRC Press, 2014.

Daniel J. Solove   *Nothing to Hide: The False Tradeoff Between Privacy and Security.* New Haven, CT: Yale University Press, 2011.

Adriana de Souza e Silva and Jordan Frith   *Mobile Interfaces in Public Spaces: Locational Privacy, Control, and Urban Sociability.* New York: Routledge, 2012.

Patrick Tucker   *The Naked Future: What Happens in a World That Anticipates Your Every Move?* New York: Current, 2014.

Robin Tudge   *The No-Nonsense Guide to Global Surveillance.* Toronto: Between the Lines, 2011.

Periodicals and Internet Sources

Brad Allenby	"The Golden Age of Privacy Is Over, But Drones Aren't to Blame," *Slate*, April 30, 2013. www.slate.com.
Julia Angwin	"US Terrorism Agency to Tap a Vast Database of Citizens," *Wall Street Journal*, December 13, 2012.
Ronald Bailey	"Your Cellphone Is Spying on You," *Reason*, vol. 44, no. 8, January 2013.
James Bamford	"The NSA Is Building the Country's Biggest Spy Center (Watch What You Say)," *Wired*, April 2012.
David Brin	"Lessons for an Age of Transparency," *New Perspectives Quarterly*, July 22, 2013.
Rosa Brooks	"Privacy Is a Red Herring: The Debate over NSA Surveillance Is About Something Else Entirely," *Foreign Policy*, November 7, 2013.
Zoë Carpenter	"What Obama Didn't Say in His Speech on NSA Spying," *Nation*, January 17, 2014.
Charles C.W. Cooke	"An Overreach for the NSA's Critics," *National Review Online*, January 13, 2014. www.nationalreview.com.
Conor Friedersdorf	"The Dangerous, False Trade-Off Between Liberty and Security," *Atlantic*, August 23, 2012.

Barton Gellman, Julie Tate, and Ashkan Soltani   "In NSA-Intercepted Data, Those Not Targeted Far Outnumber the Foreigners Who Are," *Washington Post*, July 5, 2014.

Glenn Greenwald   "Domestic Drones and Their Unique Dangers," *Guardian* (UK), March 29, 2013.

Pierre Hines   "Learn to Stop Worrying and Love the Drones," *Daily Beast*, September 17, 2013. www.thedailybeast.com.

Marcia Hofmann, Rainey Reitman, and Cindy Cohn   "2012: When the Government Comes Knocking, Who Has Your Back?," Electronic Frontier Foundation, May 31, 2012. www.eff.org.

Orin Kerr   "Why Your Cell Phone's Location Isn't Protected by the Fourth Amendment," *New Yorker*, August 5, 2013.

Alex Kozinski and Eric S. Nguyen   "Has Technology Killed the Fourth Amendment?," *Cato Supreme Court Review*, 2012. www.cato.org.

Steven Kurlander   "Domestic Surveillance: Spy vs. Spy, American vs. American," *Huffington Post*, March 13, 2013. www.huffingtonpost.com.

Steven Levy   "How the NSA Almost Killed the Internet," *Wired*, January 7, 2014.

Hugo Miller   "NSA Spying Sends Data Clients North of the Border," Bloomberg Business, January 9, 2014. www.bloomberg.com.

Anna Mulrine — "Drones over America: Public Safety Benefit or 'Creepy' Privacy Threat?," *Christian Science Monitor*, March 13, 2013.

Andrew Napolitano — "Where Is the Outrage over the Domestic Use of Drones?," Reason.com, June 7, 2012. www.reason.com.

Nick Paumgarten — "Here's Looking at You: Should We Worry About the Rise of the Drone?," *New Yorker*, May 14, 2012.

Dinah PoKempner — "Privacy in the Age of Surveillance," Foreign Policy in Focus, February 17, 2014. www.fpif.org.

Eric Posner — "Keep Spying on Foreigners, NSA," *Slate*, November 14, 2013. www.slate.com.

Glenn Harlan Reynolds — "NSA Spying Undermines Separation of Powers," *USA Today*, February 10, 2014.

Neil M. Richards — "The Dangers of Surveillance," *Harvard Law Review*, May 2013.

Gary Schmitt — "Privacy or Security: A False Choice," *Weekly Standard*, vol. 19, no. 20, February 3, 2014.

Bruce Schneier — "How the NSA Threatens National Security," *Atlantic*, January 6, 2014.

Daniel J. Solove — "Why Privacy Matters Even If You Have 'Nothing to Hide,'" *Chronicle Review*, May 15, 2011.

David Von Drehle   "The Surveillance Society," *Time*,
                    August 1, 2013.

Joe Wolverton II   "Fourth Amendment and Foreigners:
                    Does It Apply?," *New American*,
                    November 22, 2013.
                    www.thenewamerican.com.

Index

O

Obama, Barack
  bulk surveillance programs,
    72, 131, 135, 142
  FAA reauthorization, 121
  national security *vs.* right to
    freedom, 25, 83–84
  overview, 117
  public support for surveil-
    lance, 33
  surveillance checks and bal-
    ances, 98, 99
The Onion Router (TOR), 37
Open-Source software, 34–37

P

paranoia over domestic surveillance, 24–25
Paris terrorist attacks (2015), 16
Pauley, William H., 141
Pew Research Center, 18–23, 31–
  33, 115
PGP (Pretty Good Privacy) encryption, 41
phone theft, 155
Pilon, Roger, 83–85
political motives of surveillance,
  21–23
President's Review Group, 105
PRISM program, 28, 66
Privacy and Civil Liberties Oversight Board, 86–95
privacy and security
  balance between, 64–67,
    92–93
  Church Committee, 64–66
  communication privacy, 59–60
  disagreement of impact,
    48–49

government monitoring programs, 49
government surveillance and,
  47–48
NSA threat to, 51–57
overview, 44
personal concerns, 46, 115–
  116
public perceptions of, 44–50
secrecy concerns, 46–47
security, safety, and protection
  concepts, 44–46
See also Internet privacy/
  surveillance
Protect America Act (2007), 90, 99
public law principle, 126–127

R

reasonable articulable suspicion
  (RAS), 91–92, 104–106, 132, 135
Reid, Harry, 27
Review Group, 140–142
Rice, Condoleezza, 36
Ricochet.com, 109
Rogers, Mike, 72–73
rule of law, 150–151

S

safeguards against domestic surveillance, 34–38
Schell, Jonathan, 96–100
Schneier, Bruce, 58, 61
secondary inspections, 69–70
secret law, 125–126
Section 702 program, 94–95
security, safety, and protection
  concepts, 44–46
self-searching activity, 48

V

Verton, Dan, 24–26

W

warrantless surveillance, 90
Washington Post-ABC News polls,
    16, 32, 115
The Washington Post newspaper,
    116

Whisper Systems, 38
WikiLeaks, 100
Wiretap Act (1968), 15
wiretapping, 80, 118
Wyden, Ron, 99, 123–130

Z

Zazi, Najibullah, 75, 85
Zuckerman, Jessica, 118–122